Cruising southbound on the Siskiyou Line, SP SD9 #4330 leads a sister SD9 (in "Kodachrome" merger paint) and a long string of empty cars, as the Yoncalla Local rolls past semaphore signal towers near Creswell, Oregon, May 1989.

Backwoods Railroads

Branchlines and Shortlines of Western Oregon

D. C. Jesse Burkhardt

Washington State University Press
Pullman, Washington

Washington State University Press, Pullman, Washington 99164-5910

Printed and bound in the United States of America on low pH, low acid, high
quality recycled paper. ✪

Library of Congress Cataloging-in-Publication Data

Burkhardt, D. C. Jesse, 1953-
    Backwoods railroads : branchlines & shortlines of western Oregon /
D.C. Jesse Burkhardt.
      p.   cm.
    Includes bibliographical references and index.
    ISBN 0-87422-104-8
    1. Railroads--Oregon.   I. Title.
TF24.07B87   1994
385' .09795 -- dc20   93-42338
                                                       CIP

To Jane
For believing in the book.

CONTENTS

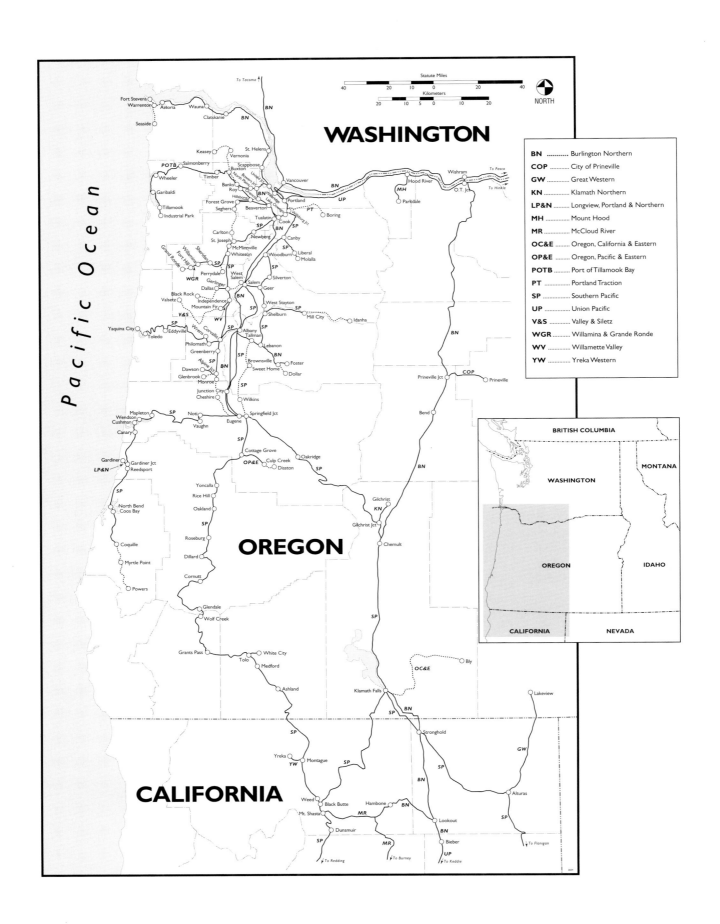

A Point in Time: Oregon Railroading in the 1990s

A Word from the WSU Press

In *Backwoods Railroads*, D.C. Jesse Burkhardt gives us an engaging description of contemporary branchline operations in western Oregon. His focus is on the Willamette Valley and its bordering mountains—the Coast Range, Cascades, and Siskiyous. As he so aptly points out, this region is "the economic heart of the state." Its intricate "railroad network is the closest Oregon comes to the kind of trackage density found in many Eastern and Midwestern states."

Historically, small companies undertook much of the railway building in western Oregon, intending to make profits hauling Willamette Valley passengers and farm produce as well as tapping lumber operations in the foothills and mountains. Passenger service has long since disappeared on these lines, but little else has changed in the orientation of rail traffic. Today, as at the turn of the century, trains roll along the tracks serving agricultural and lumber shippers. Some of these lines are short indeed, extending just several miles off a Burlington Northern or Southern Pacific mainline.

Burkhardt completed most of the research for *Backwoods Railroads* between 1989 and early 1993, and he depicts western Oregon's branchlines and shortlines as they operated at that time. An *Oregon Business* magazine associate editor with a keen interest in the railroad industry, he is intimately familiar with virtually all of the lines he writes about. Furthermore, Burkhardt's unique photojournalistic style effectively captures a sense of Oregon's rural, small-town character and heritage. All photographs in this book are Burkhardt's, unless otherwise indicated.

As in all human endeavors, time and change march on, and this certainly is true of the railroad business. Because of the economic and regulatory conditions, large carriers across the nation are leasing or selling branchlines, while maintaining their mainlines to serve the small carriers that are taking over operations on feeder trackage. This scenario is true for western Oregon as well.

A particularly significant event in this regard occurred on February 22, 1993, while this book was in preparation. On that day, the Southern Pacific signed a lease agreement with newcomer Willamette & Pacific Railroad, and, shortly thereafter, the W&P began handling operations on several SP shortlines described in this book. SP owns more than 700 miles of western Oregon branchlines; the Willamette & Pacific took over operations on 184 miles of this trackage. Another hundred miles of SP branches likewise were leased or sold to other shortline haulers on the same date. This trend is likely to continue, affecting additional lines outlined in this book.

Word of the Southern Pacific lease agreements came too late for the author and the WSU Press to update those sections of the book describing the lines affected by the changes. However, day to day activities on these lines have remained largely the same—whether the locomotive on the point displays the SP letters, or the W&P, or some other shortline logo. Burkhardt briefly updates the reader about these and other recent changes in western Oregon's shortline network in the epilogue at the end of the text.

Here, then, is a look at contemporary branchline and shortline operations in this unique region as of early 1993. The book is profusely illustrated, and crafted with an attention to detail. We invite you to enjoy railroad writing at its best.

The Editors

A canopy of colorful trees and the trestle over the Marys River frame the northbound
Dawson Local, swaying back to Corvallis on the Southern Pacific's West Side Branch.
Although the date is October 18, 1990, and the power is diesel—SP SD9 #4399—the
hole the right-of-way has created through the trees appears to be a plume of steam.

INTRODUCTION

Train whistle cries
lost on its own track
I close my eyes
I ain't never comin' back . . .

—Dave Alvin, "Long White Cadillac"

©1983 Twin Duck Music BMI

At isolated Alpine Junction, the seldom-used Southern Pacific tracks curve west toward the misty Coast Range mountains. Two times a week, on Tuesdays and Thursdays, a single locomotive rumbles south from Corvallis with two or three or four empty freight cars bound for a backwoods (literally) lumber mill in Dawson, about 23 miles away. A couple of hours later, back the engine comes with two or three or four loads of lumber and woodchips. The train's operations seem so basic, so pure.

On Mondays, Wednesdays, and Fridays, the same three-member crew takes the same locomotive and goes in the other direction from Corvallis. Beginning at 6 a.m., they prepare a cut of cars and clatter north through the Willamette Valley to Dallas, on a route that traverses rich farmlands and the wine-producing region around Independence. Along the way, the train rolls through V&S Junction, a once busy interchange point with the Willamette Valley Railroad.

Passing grain silos that stand like silent sentinels over rusting sidings in a lonely countryside, the northbound Dallas Local follows the West Side Branch for 25 miles to reach Gerlinger Junction.

Gerlinger is a nondescript place, like so many of the stations along this backwater route. There are no structures there, no homes, no silos, no lights even; simply a switch stand and a wye that allows access onto the 5.3-mile Dallas Branch. To the west of Gerlinger Junction is the railhead in Dallas, and the line's primary shipper: Willamette Industries' sawmill, good for a dozen cars of lumber each week. To the east, the rails have been removed from ten miles of roadbed that once reached into Salem, Oregon's capital city.

These scenes are microcosms of rural railroading across Oregon. But these peaceful slices of Oregon's heritage are getting scarcer with each passing year. Across the nation, countless stretches of track are being scrapped, torn from the land whereupon they've rested for decades.

As a youngster growing up in Jackson, Michigan, during the 1960s, I listened to New York Central freight trains rolling into the night, air horns blowing at grade crossings as they rumbled southwest out of town. Lying in bed beside my open window, not wanting to sleep, I heard those trains moving on the NYC's fast "Air Line" tracks. Beyond the subdivisions and across the fields, they were on their way to Lime Lake and Concord and Three Rivers; bulling toward the state line and eventually to a large rail terminal at Elkhart in north-central Indiana. From there, trains continued out of the Farm Belt to an unimagined index of geographic possibilities. That seemed fascinating, the wonder of those distant points—the magic of the Midwestern plains and the continent beyond.

By rail, one could get from Jackson, Michigan, to Tillamook, Oregon, or Mattawamkeag, Maine, or Gila, Arizona, or Sioux Lookout, Ontario, or any one of thousands of trackside towns. In that sense, all of

The author in Eugene.
Photo: Jane C. Burkhardt.

our communities were tied together by those twin steel bands and their timber and gravel roadbeds. It is akin to a spiritual connection, something that a mere highway could never match.

In 1984, the mainline railroad near my home of so many years in Jackson—the line my mother had warned me to avoid when I was a boy, the line I had later walked along to and from high school nearly every day, the line I had thought would be in use throughout my lifetime—was abandoned.

"Unnecessary mileage," a Conrail spokesman explained. By 1985 the once-vital rails and ties had been removed, leaving merely a path of gravel and dirt through the trees. It's a heartbreaking sight that has become increasingly common across North America.

Throughout Oregon, the names of "outback" railroad stations read as if they belong in an atlas of obscure places: Tolo. Mountain Fir. Ashahr. Minto. Siltcoos. Canary. Narrows. Suver. Dry Creek. Timber. All that links these places is a network of remote rail lines. And as obscure as these locations are, they would be even more obscure without the railroads—if they existed at all. Many towns in Oregon can trace their beginnings to the whims of railroad presidents and their surveyors decades ago. As a result of decisions made generations ago, the convenient rail line through a community provides an economic gateway to markets in distant states.

In the 1990s, a freight train rolling over a middle-of-nowhere feeder track on its way to or from a rural railroad town is almost an anachronism. These lines host one train a day or two trains a week—trains that roll to almost forgotten towns in the backwoods of western Oregon's countryside. The branches and shortlines are evolving. Routes are drying up, being taken out of service, sold or leased to new owners. Many routes are endangered, and once gone will be gone forever.

The overall condition of Oregon's branchline trackage is not reassuring. Largely as a result of feeder track abandonments, Oregon's railroad network has fallen from 3,560 miles in 1973 to 2,600 miles in 1992, while employment in the industry statewide has tumbled from 7,500 workers in 1978 to fewer than 3,500 in 1992.

I feel it is important to preserve a piece of what remains, via text and photographs, by providing a contemporary "snapshot" of some of Oregon's rail operations in the late 1980s and early 1990s. Even in the relatively short time I've been working on this book (approximately five years), there have been dramatic changes in Oregon. These include the abandonment of the 65-mile Oregon, California & Eastern, one of the West's last logging roads; and the scrapping of the Portland Traction line between Portland (Golf Junction) and Boring. Also, 90 miles of Southern Pacific's Tillamook Branch has been sold to a shortline operator. There will almost certainly be more changes before *Backwoods Railroads* reaches the bookstores.

In previous decades, fine books on Oregon railroads have been written by authors such as Edwin D. Culp, who produced *Stations West* in 1972, and Randall V. Mills, author of the superb *Railroads down the Valleys* in 1950. More recently, in 1987, Ed Austin and Tom Dill put together *The Southern Pacific in Oregon.* Theirs is a worthy tradition of solid reporting that I hope to carry on with *Backwoods Railroads: Branchlines and Shortlines of Western Oregon.* There isn't a lot of time left for some of these lines, and I want them to be remembered. 🚂

D. C. Jesse Burkhardt
Lake Oswego, Oregon
January 3, 1993

Gerlinger Junction, Oregon, in July 1990. Here the Dallas Branch and West Side Branch join. In this view, looking west toward the Coast Range mountains, a broken down telegrapher's shanty and telegraph pole remain, even after the diamond and track that once extended due east to Salem have been removed, leaving only a few castoff sections of rail behind. Straight ahead is the remnant of the Dallas Branch: five miles of track that leads to Dallas. The West Side Branch runs north-south through Gerlinger. There is a wye just off to the right of this view that allows access onto the branch. The huge grain silo down the track is owned by the Dallas Co-op; they no longer ship by rail.

CHAPTER 1

BACKWARD ALONG THE BAILEY BRANCH

Southern Pacific's lower West Side Branch,
Bailey Branch, and Wilkins Branch

All but forgotten at the northwestern edge of Southern Pacific Transportation Company's far-flung "Golden Empire" is an inconspicuous stretch of track that carries the Dawson Local. The train works out of Corvallis along a hook-shaped route made up of segments of two SP branchlines to serve a small sawmill in Dawson, 23 miles by rail from Corvallis. Dawson is the western terminus of the 6.9-mile Bailey Branch, and the freight train that operates over it exists, primarily, to transport the products of a lone customer: Hull-Oakes Lumber Company, a rail-dependent facility that makes specialty, large dimension wooden beams.

There are a handful of other intermittently active stations along the route, and even their names—Greenberry, Dry Creek, Alpine Junction—tend to inspire images of Oregon's outback. Shippers at these places move commodities such as grass seed, Christmas trees, and recycled newspaper, but their combined total comprises no more than 5 percent of the tonnage moving over these two lines in a given year. Clearly, it's what's coming out of Dawson that keeps trains rolling past their loading docks.

As a point of reference, wood and paper products have accounted for roughly 80 percent of SP's Oregon haulage, and traffic on this route reflects that: it's almost entirely lumber and woodchips. And although the economic health of the forest products industry has been in decline in Oregon in the 1980s and

1990s, the manufacture of lumber and wood products remains one of the state's key industries. Approximately 62,000 Oregon workers were employed in the manufacture of wood and paper products in 1992.

Furthermore, a large share of Oregon's lumber shipments—35 percent in 1992, according to the Western Wood Products Association—travels to market by railroad. Given that fact, the need for a healthy rail transportation system can hardly be overstated, and Oregon is fortunate to be served by three large and relatively prosperous carriers: Burlington Northern, Union Pacific, and Southern Pacific. All operate long stretches of fast, modern mainline.

To reach the Hull-Oakes sawmill at Dawson, a train leaves the small classification yard in Corvallis and travels south to Alpine Junction on a part of the 66-mile West Side Branch. The 17.3-mile section of West Side trackage straight south of Corvallis to where the line ends in Monroe is commonly referred to as the "lower West Side." (In the other direction, the West Side Branch once extended as far north as Hillsboro, 93 miles from Monroe, but the line is now segmented—see chapter seven.) The West Side Branch connects with the Bailey Branch at Alpine Junction.

On its journey back and forth from Corvallis, the Dawson Local—also known as the Corvallis Local—tours through some of Benton County's finest farm country. The train passes ranchlands astir with grazing sheep, skirts the boundaries of the William L. Finley National Wildlife Refuge, and touches the shadow of Marys Peak, at 4,097 feet the highest point in the Coast Range. The run is flat and uncommonly straight. After crossing a short steel and timber trestle over the Marys River, directly south of Corvallis,

Near Bailey on the Bailey Branch, July 17, 1990. As the Dawson Local is on its way back to home base in Corvallis, a mishap occurs: the wheels of the two cars directly behind SD9 #4314 have slipped off the track. The crew patiently waits in 90-degree heat for help coming from Corvallis.

March 19, 1991: the Dawson Local is switching the Hull-Oakes Lumber Company sawmill at the end of the 6.9-mile Bailey Branch.

Bailey Branch (SP)
Stations

Alpine Junction .... MP 673.0
Dawson .... MP 679.9

the track doesn't curve again until reaching a point south of Alpine Junction—some 15 miles of pure tangent, with hardly an undulation.

A little over a mile south of Alpine Junction is Monroe, a tiny town where freight service is seldom required. A feed mill, Willamette Seed & Grain, is located at rail's end there. The company used to bring in an occasional hopper load of fertilizer, but now its spur is disconnected.

Many years ago, Monroe was just another way station on the West Side line from Corvallis to Eugene. Until 1932, daily passenger trains connected the two college towns, as the branch reached south via Cheshire and Monroe and eventually joined with SP's Coos Bay Branch at Transfer, a few miles west of Eugene. The stretch of track south of Monroe, to

Cheshire, however, was abandoned in the 1950s.

Though the terrain is unchallenging, a road unit is employed, normally an SD9, to handle the Dawson Local, and freight movements south of Corvallis are almost always headed by a single locomotive. There is little need for extra power on this route, given the flatness of the terrain and the paucity of carloads, with anywhere from two to seven or eight cars per train being typical.

At Alpine Junction, trains bound for Dawson are switched from the West Side Branch onto the Bailey Branch itself, heading west and deeper into the Oregon woods. Oddly, the train serving the Bailey Branch rolls *backward*—caboose first—the entire 6.9 miles from Alpine Junction to the Hull-Oakes mill. (This backing move insures that cabooses will continue to be seen on the branch, as a crew member is required to stand on the rear platform of the caboose to spy the right-of-way.) Backing the train is necessitated by the track configuration at the Hull-Oakes end-of-branch facility: there is no yard, no wye, nor even a siding there—only three dead-end spur tracks.

To reassemble for the backing move to Dawson,

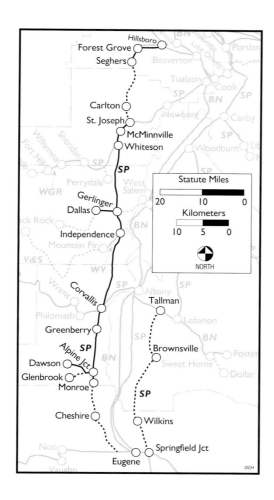

Southern Pacific's West Side Branch, Bailey Branch,
Dallas Branch, and Wilkins Branch

the locomotive leads the entire train onto the siding at Alpine Junction. The engine then cuts off from the rest of the train, moves forward to the southern end of the siding, and returns on the main track. It then retrieves the caboose from the rear of the string, and pushes it onto Bailey Branch trackage. Then the engine picks up the rest of the freight cars, and couples them onto the caboose. After this process is completed, the SD9 slowly shoves the train in reverse all the way to Dawson, alongside pristine vineyards that spread over the rolling hills beside the tracks.

At the end of the rails is Hull-Oakes' steam powered sawmill, built a half-century ago. Besides using old-fashioned, steam-driven milling equipment, Hull-Oakes also has one of the few remaining wigwam kilns still operating in the state. Most significantly, Hull-Oakes is reported to be the last mill in the United States that can cut dimension timbers up to 85 feet long, and as such the company fills orders from all over the world. This capability, however, has become somewhat paradoxical: if the direct rail connection is lost, the mill would almost certainly be forced to close, displacing more than 80 employees. As tight as the current lumber market is, trying to haul specialty products to a mainline reload site would not only be impractical, it could leave Hull-Oakes uncompetitive. The rail link is crucial.

When the train arrives at Dawson, the caboose is shoved onto one of Hull-Oakes' industrial spurs. Then the engine gathers loaded flatcars and woodchip cars, and leaves empties in their place. After switching operations are completed, the freight cars

West Side Branch (SP)
Stations

are coupled back onto the caboose and the train is ready to pull ahead—this time facing forward.

Given the speed restrictions on the line—10 mph on the Bailey Branch, 20 mph on the lower West Side—simply getting to Dawson and back takes most of the crew's time. Including the unusual switching procedure at Alpine Junction and spotting cars at Dawson, it takes six to eight hours to complete Bailey Branch chores. It's a full day's work by the time the crew gets back to the Corvallis freight office.

Unfortunately, there apparently hasn't been enough tonnage moving off the Bailey Branch to make it profitable enough for SP to operate. This is especially true considering that a significant portion of Hull-Oakes carloads are revenue-poor woodchip shipments being short-hauled to the Georgia-Pacific mill in Toledo. Railroads generally make their living carrying expensive cargoes long distances, and wood-chips out of Dawson bound for Toledo don't qualify in either category.

Yet there are seasonal increases in the number of carloadings off the lower West Side Branch. For example, shipments of grass seed from a number of businesses in Greenberry and Dry Creek are concen-

trated in the summer months (when "Railbox" cars become a frequent sight). And there is plenty of seed to be distributed, as more than 90 percent of the grass seed produced in the United States comes from the Willamette Valley. In late autumn, the Holiday Tree Farms Company assembles a large crew of laborers and invades the quiescence of Alpine Junction. There, during November and December, freshly cut Christmas trees are sorted, stacked, and loaded into refrigerated boxcars and trucks for shipment nationwide. The southern part of Benton County has been termed "the Christmas tree capital of the world," and for at least a month or two each year, business is good.

Backing toward Dawson on March 1, 1990, SP's Dawson Local crosses a short trestle with SD9 #4333 doing the pushing.

Also, directly south of SP's Corvallis switching yard, a spur track leads to the Evanite Fiber Corporation industrial complex. Evanite's Corvallis operations include a battery separator facility and a hardboard mill.

The fact that this low-density, lightly built, branchline track has survived at all makes it something special. The lower West Side and Bailey branchlines carry less than 1 million tons annually; and Oregon Department of Transportation figures reveal that only about 600 carloads (not counting Evanite's) a year move over these two segments.

So, how does a branchline with only 75-lb. rail and a traffic base of woodchips, lumber, Christmas trees, and grass seed manage to survive? One clue: it helps to have a lot of friends.

In May 1985, SP placed the lower West Side and Bailey Branch in "Category 1": subject to abandonment within three years. Southern Pacific also placed the entire Bailey Branch in what is termed an "excepted" classification—meaning that maintenance is held to a bare, as-needed minimum, and trains are not allowed to move any faster than 10 mph.

The entire stretch of track linking Dawson and Monroe to Corvallis is 75-lb. rail, using crushed rock ballast between Dawson and Alpine Junction and pit run between Monroe and Corvallis. It's not in bad shape, although the deferred maintenance will of course catch up to it eventually. In fairness to Southern Pacific, it should be noted that even basic maintenance costs on a low-density branch can total between $3,000 and $7,000 a mile, per year. For a line such as the Bailey Branch—with just one significant shipper—that can be a high, even prohibitive, cost for a carrier to bear, especially for relatively few carloads a month.

Thus, the route to Dawson is regarded as endangered ("highly endangered," according to the Oregon Public Utility Commission) yet it continues to show resilience. Indeed, preservation of the West Side and Bailey branchlines might be considered a contemporary model of how to keep service intact.

An abandonment application for the Corvallis-Monroe segment of the West Side Branch, along with the entire Bailey Branch, was filed by SP with the Interstate Commerce Commission (ICC) on March 31, 1986. Fortunately for the lumber mill in Dawson and the handful of shippers along the lower West Side Line, SP's abandonment application included trackage into an industrial park located adjacent to the Corvallis Municipal Airport a few miles south of Corvallis. This prompted the city of Corvallis (population 43,000), as well as officials of Benton County, where all of the trackage is located, to become perhaps even more aggressively involved in protesting the application than they might otherwise have been. Business leaders in the community had been actively promoting industrial sites to attract rail users—and job providers—to the area, and they were not happy about the possibility of seeing the track torn out.

No less than 28 protests were filed against SP's petition. Included were not only *every* shipper and potential shipper along the line, but a lot of big guns: the mayors of Monroe and Corvallis, the Corvallis Chamber of Commerce, the Oregon Department of Transportation, the Oregon Public Utility Commission, and several state legislators. Even Pacific Power & Light offered its assistance, as the utility considers preservation of this trackage to be an important factor in regional economic development.

And unlike some branchline shippers who accepted abandonment as "inevitable," and allowed them-

West Side Branch (SP)
Direct Traffic Control Blocks

Wellsdale Block	West MP 691.0; East MP 699.2
Independence Block	West MP 699.2; East MP 709.0
Derry Block	West MP 709.0; East MP 715.0
McCoy Block	West MP 715.0; East MP 722.8
Amity Block	West MP 722.8; East MP 730.0

selves to be seduced by the short-term savings a trucking firm offered, Hull-Oakes didn't give up on the railroad. Wayne Giesy, the sawmill's sales manager, saw to it that Hull-Oakes transported all it possibly could by rail, and he also met with other on-line shippers and encouraged them to take delivery by rail as opposed to truck whenever possible. This helped to keep carloadings at a reasonably consistent level.

The numerous responses against abandonment were filed on June 23, 1986. In the face of this strong display of interest in retaining the lines—and to the company's credit—SP lost little time in withdrawing the abandonment application, doing so just two weeks later on July 7.

The importance of the community's determination was not lost on Claudia Howells, deputy assistant commissioner of the Public Utility Commission. In a letter to the author, she wrote: "We developed a tremendous fondness for the Bailey Branch, due mostly to Wayne Giesy and Hull-Oakes Lumber Company, but also because of the dedication of many other Benton County people." In unity, strength.

Frequency of service on the line, however, has dropped substantially in the past decade. In 1978, there was a local that pulled out of Corvallis bound for Dawson and Monroe at high noon every weekday. By 1985, trains rolled south down the valley just three times a week. The level of business in the early 1990s calls for two trains weekly. (On the other three days of the week, the crew goes north of Corvallis as the "Dallas Local"—see chapter seven.)

All cars moving to and from shippers along the Bailey Branch and the lower West Side are routed over SP's heavy-density mainline—it carries more than 20 million gross tons of freight per year—via Albany, 12 miles northeast of Corvallis and reached by way of the relatively busy Toledo Branch. SP's

Above—Southern Pacific SD9 #4431 working the Hull-Oakes Lumber Company sawmill at Dawson, February 16, 1988.

Below—SD9 #4410 swings past the 10 mph speed board at Alpine Junction as it returns from the Hull-Oakes sawmill. The sun lights up new grass springing up in the rich agricultural acreage of south Benton County.

Wilkins Branch; SP SD9 #4336 returns with two flats from the Bohemia mill at Wilkins. The Wilkins Branch was abandoned in December 1985, and the tracks were pulled up shortly thereafter.
Photo: Scott Anderson.

Albany Yard is an important sorting facility for several local trains.

The future for the West Side and Bailey branchlines is as unsettled as their history is intriguing. Most railway construction west of the Cascade Range was carried out by small railroads hoping to earn profits by hauling passengers and agricultural products into and out of the Willamette Valley, as well as providing an outlet for logging operations in the foothills and mountains. In this respect, although passenger service has long since been dropped on these routes, not much else has changed in the orientation of rail freight service. In the 1990s, as in the 1890s, trains move to serve shippers of agricultural and lumber products.

The Willamette Valley is located between the Coast and Cascade ranges, a wide geographic region that holds some of North America's most spectacular and productive forests. The area represents the economic heart of the state, and its railroad network is the closest Oregon comes to the kind of trackage density found in many Eastern and Midwestern states. The lush valley not only holds the main north-south trunk lines, highway and rail, through Oregon, but also forms a key segment of the great "West Coast Transportation Corridor" that stretches from Vancouver, British Columbia, to San Diego, California.

At one time there were a total of four alternate, basically parallel railways running through the Willamette Valley linking Eugene and Portland; redundancy that over the decades has been pared to two: Burlington Northern's Oregon Electric Branch and SP's hectic mainline that slices through the center of the valley and, appropriately, is known as the Valley Line.

The name "West Side Branch" originated from the basic geography of its route: the track traverses the western side of the Willamette Valley, and was built west of the original Oregon & California Railroad mainline—now SP's Valley Line. The West Side Branch came into being as an expansion south of Portland. By way of McMinnville and Independence, rails reached Corvallis in 1879 as part of the Western Oregon Railroad Company. The Western Oregon soon became part of the Oregon & California Railroad, and was briefly known as the O&C, Westside Division. The track was built to move, among other things, wheat that previously had been shipped on Willamette River steamboats. Remnants of the old tracks to long-gone loading docks on the Willamette River are still visible in places along the riverfront in Corvallis.

Trackage south of Corvallis that now forms the route of the Dawson Local was built in 1908-1909 as part of Stephen Carver's Corvallis & Alsea River Railway Company, a line he intended to take all the way to the Pacific Coast. But Carver's inability in 1909 to secure sufficient financial credit prevented the line from being completed, and only about 30 miles was laid. In 1911, the Corvallis & Alsea River was purchased by the Portland, Eugene & Eastern Railway, which in turn was sold to Southern Pacific in 1912.

Although SP still calls the line between Alpine Junction and Dawson the "Bailey Branch," there is little to justify it. Bailey, located roughly five miles east of Dawson, is a true ghost station. There is no

Wilkins Branch (SP); abandoned 1985
Stations

Springfield
Coburg
Wilkins
Bowers
Rowland
Brownsville
Plainview
Tallman

shipper there, and no siding; nothing except a big farmhouse on a nearby rise. In fact, the station known as Bailey is not even listed in SP's timetable any longer, nor in the *Official Railway Guide* station index. For some reason, however, Rand McNally still includes Bailey in its latest *Handy Railroad Atlas of the United States.*

The station became important because there was once a short stretch of track leading southwest from Bailey to a lumber mill in Glenbrook; at that time the station served a real purpose, and was known as Bailey Junction. The town of Alpine (hence Alpine Junction) was also located on the Glenbrook extension. In the 1920s, passenger service from these isolated towns to Eugene or Corvallis was available every day except Sunday. The Glenbrook track was abandoned decades ago, and today there is scarcely a trace of the old roadbed. But the line's identification with Bailey Junction remains.

The successful defense of a threatened low density rail link such as the Bailey Branch is good news for the state of Oregon. By way of contrast, however, it is instructive to remember the fate of another SP segment—the Wilkins Branch—not too many miles away across the Willamette Valley floor. Considered a "mirror image" of the lower West Side/Bailey Branch, the line reached south from Tallman, through Brownsville, to the Bohemia lumber mill in Wilkins. That right-of-way has been reduced to splintered remnants of creosote-stained ties, along with a few spikes the scrappers neglected, and it needn't have come to that. In fact, the Wilkins Branch story appears to be a poignant lesson in how to *forfeit* rail service.

Neither SP nor the ICC was overly impressed with

SD9 #4402 switches cars in Dallas on October 5, 1990. After leaving Dallas, the train will return south to Corvallis via Independence. A crew based in Corvallis handles both the Dawson Local and the Dallas Local on alternating days.

the handful of less-than-spirited protests filed against the Wilkins Branch abandonment application. Some marginal businesses on the line promised to send statements, but for whatever reason did not. And the main shipper, Bohemia, simply resubmitted its 1978 dissent against an earlier SP abandonment petition, wherein it had outlined plans to expand mill operations if rail service was retained. In the intervening seven years, Bohemia still had not expanded, and so it was not surprising that Southern Pacific branded Bohemia's 1978 objections "irrelevant" in 1985. The ICC agreed with Southern Pacific, and allowed the abandonment.

It should be pointed out that, also stacked against preservation of the Wilkins line, was the extremely poor condition of its ancient physical plant—62-lb. rail installed in the early 1900s, with ties in poor condition. And carloadings were considerably lower than on the Bailey Branch, with just 184 cars in 1984, the last full year of service on the segment. That's not much revenue for a 30-mile line, and even that anemic figure was down sharply from the previous year's 268 carloads. It can almost be said that Wilkins Branch shippers abandoned the track in effect before Southern Pacific did so in fact. In any event, in December 1985, operations were halted; the track was pulled up in early 1986. As a result, significant expansion of Bohemia's Wilkins plant (now owned by Willamette Industries) might be a less attractive option, and the town of Brownsville has been stripped of direct rail service.

There's a quote from the recommendations of the Oregon Governor's Task Force on Rail Line Abandonments (released by the Public Utility Commission in October 1986) that is worth tacking on a wall somewhere. It reads:

> The only reasonable method of assuring long-term direct rail service on railroad branch lines is to maintain or increase traffic levels and decrease operating costs to a point capable of supporting the operation of the line without public subsidy.

A non-legislated solution to the dispute over closures of rural branchlines seems to be taking shape. Due to changing market and regulatory conditions, Southern Pacific announced its desire to sell or lease, rather than abandon, light-traffic branches in Oregon. Other large carriers nationwide are pursuing a similar course. (By the early 1990s, SP operated 15 branchline segments in the state, totaling over 700 miles.)

Public-relations gains in the wake of SP's January 1986 sale of the 55-mile Lakeview Branch (from Alturas, California, to Lakeview, Oregon) have further encouraged SP to seek shortline operators as a preferred alternative to quick abandonment. The Lakeview Branch was purchased by Oregon's Lake County to preserve service to several lumber mills in Lakeview, and is being operated by the Colorado based Great Western Railway. The Great Western moved a total of 623 cars over the line in 1992.

In another positive development, the new owners of the 21-mile-long Mount Hood Railroad have rejuvenated a former Union Pacific branch that stretches south from Hood River—where it connects with the Union Pacific—to Parkdale. The Mount Hood was originally an independent shortline that began service in 1906. It was purchased by UP in 1968, and sold to a group of investors—including the line's major shippers—in 1987. Primary products moving over this line include lumber and fruit from

A crew member of SP's Dawson Local makes sure all is in order before the train leaves Corvallis for the day's switching assignments.

the rich Hood River Valley, along with occasional shipments of liquefied petroleum gas and lime. The shortline handled a total of 604 cars in 1992. Passenger excursion trains also are proving to be a successful generator of supplemental income.

Rail transportation remains of special interest to Oregon shippers, not only because of the natural resource base of so many Oregon products, but also due to the state's geographic isolation from important markets. Extremely promising for shippers throughout Southern Pacific's extensive Oregon network was the October 1988 sale of Southern Pacific to the Denver & Rio Grande Western Railroad. The Rio Grande has declared its intent to aggressively serve the Northwest's lumber industry, and many business leaders statewide are excited at the prospect of one-carrier service all the way to St. Louis and Chicago. (SP gained its long-desired access to Chicago on November 8, 1989, by purchasing the Chicago, Missouri & Western Railway's St. Louis-Chicago mainline.)

Bringing the Denver & Rio Grande Western into Oregon ushers an interested (and by all accounts enthusiastic) new owner onto the scene. The D&RGW has already reopened SP's Modoc Line— from Klamath Falls, Oregon, to Flanigan, Nevada, via Alturas, California—to through freights, thereby slashing 258 miles from previous east/west movements. Potential new connections and routings via the D&RGW should help to provide more competitive rates for Oregon shippers.

The backwater Bailey Branch is perhaps an anachronism. But more than eight decades after its construction, the valued rail line endures. Twice a week, local residents can still gaze upon the glowing headlamp of the train, swaying home from Dawson on its line-straight haul after the slow turn out of Alpine Junction. Thus, for now, creaking freight cars continue to move through southern Benton County, and the screech of steel wheels on rails still echoes through the slumbering rural stations there. For at least a while longer, the fresh scent of tons of wood-chips rolling out of Dawson will continue to be carried on Willamette Valley breezes.

The Dallas Local backs into the Corvallis Yard, September 19, 1990, following its return from serving the Willamette Industries lumber mill at Dallas and the Willamette Valley Railroad interchange at Independence. The locomotive will tie up in the yard for the evening and go back to work early the next morning in its alternate role as the Dawson Local.

CHAPTER 2

MOUNTAIN BRANCHLINE

*Southern Pacific's Coos Bay Branch, with connecting
shortline Longview, Portland & Northern Railway*

At a glance, the Coos Bay Branch appears on transportation maps as a thin line pointing toward Oregon's central coast. The track leads west out of the Willamette Valley, away from Southern Pacific Transportation Company's sprawling 363-acre Eugene Yard. It snakes its way through the Coast Range to the Port of Coos Bay, and continues as far south as Coquille.

One might assume the line serves a sparsely populated, perhaps economically depressed part of the state—and to an extent this is true. Unemployment remains a serious concern in the region, especially in Coos County, where unemployment rates consistently run in double figures—standing at 11.5 percent in January 1993, according to the Oregon Employment Division. Coos Bay, the key station on the branch, has a population of only 15,000. Yet Coos Bay and the area immediately surrounding it represent the largest population center on the Oregon coast, and lining the 137.4-mile route between Eugene and Coquille are a host of active lumber facilities. These factors combine to make the Coos Bay Line one of SP's best Oregon properties.

This reality is made dramatically clear by the presence of the "Coos Bay Hauler," the flagship train operating over the line. The Coos Bay Hauler moves between Eugene Yard and Coos Bay Yard with an average consist of 60 to 70 freight cars, but it's not uncommon to see 90-car freights thundering along the scenic right-of-way, headed by several locomotives. Multiple-unit lash-ups are commonplace on this branchline. In various combinations, GP40-2s,

SD9s, GP9s, and TEBU (Tractive Effort Booster Unit) slugs, rebuilt from U25Bs, mix to pull long trains through western Oregon's hilly landscape.

The impressive level of tonnage SP is hauling out of this area of the coast is solid evidence that the route is doing more than its share to meet operating expenses. Indeed, an old story still in circulation suggests that, at one time, income from business on the Coos Bay Branch *alone* generated enough revenue to pay all the bills for the entire division. That's not too surprising, considering that Southern Pacific moved nearly 16,000 cars annually over this trackage as recently as 1985. Even though the years since then have seen that figure dropping somewhat, the traffic base seems at least steady, with good potential for increasing.

The line is listed by the Federal Railroad Administration as a "Category A" branchline, meaning the route carries between 1 million and 5 million gross tons of traffic a year ("B" branchlines haul less than 1 million gross tons). Southern Pacific's only other "A" branches in the state are: the Toledo Branch (mainly serving a large Georgia-Pacific mill near the coast in Toledo, to the tune of some 20,000 cars per year—see chapter six); and the well-built Siskiyou Line (see chapter eight), which formed part of the original Oregon & California Railroad north-south mainline, and was SP's main trunk through the state until the Cascade Line opened in 1926.

Physically, the route of the Coos Bay Branch, through the Coast Range and then along the coastline, is an engineering marvel. The topography is varied and at times spectacular, and construction of the right-of-way reflects that. Between Eugene and Myrtle Point, which is located nine miles south of

The Coos Bay Hauler crosses the Umpqua River drawbridge at Reedsport, on a foggy afternoon in October 1988.

Tunnel #2 on the Coos Bay Line, 1914.
Collection of Tom Dill.

Coos Bay Branch (SP)
Stations

Coquille, nearly 36,000 feet of trestles were built, and there are numerous tunnels—including 4,183-ft.-long Tunnel #19 near Reedsport, the longest SP tunnel in Oregon.

The roadbed plant ranges from 112-lb. to 136-lb. rail, with crushed rock ballast. The route's ties are in mostly good condition. Speed limits to and from Coos Bay range from 10 to 40 mph, with the slow speed orders due to curves, tunnels, and bridges, and not necessarily for sections of bad track. The line has by no means been neglected.

There are four drawbridges on the route. At Cushman, the line crosses the Siuslaw River, where the drawspan is virtually always aligned to handle rail traffic. At Reedsport, there is a swingspan across the Umpqua River while at Cordes, the track passes over the branch's namesake, Coos Bay, on the 460-ft. North Bend Drawbridge. And directly south of Coos Bay Yard, there is a short drawbridge over Coalbank Slough. The spans at Reedsport and Cordes are normally left open for barge traffic, with a bridgetender assigned to arrive in advance of train movements to turn the bridge for rail traffic.

SP's Coos Bay Branch has the distinction of being the longest stretch of track in Oregon's coastal region. It parallels the Pacific Ocean for approximately 53 miles, from the Siuslaw River crossing at Cushman to Coos Bay Yard. Coos Bay offers the potential of

Above—SD9 #4436 leads SP's Coos Bay Hauler out of Tunnel #15 at Canary.

Left—Southern Pacific's Reedsport Drawbridge on the Coos Bay Branch.

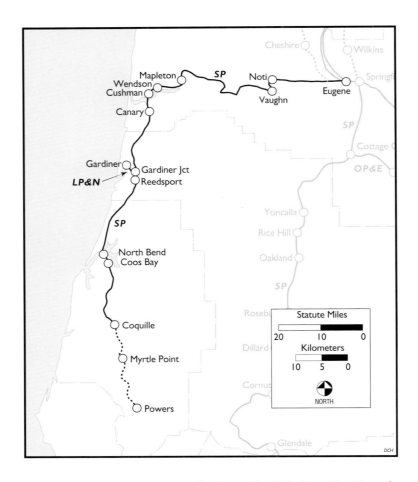

Southern Pacific's Coos Bay Branch, with connecting
shortline Longview, Portland & Northern Railway

becoming a significant West Coast port, possibly able to provide competition to high-profile terminals at Portland, Tacoma, and Seattle. At least that is the hope, although Coos Bay is limited by one substantial drawback: Coos Bay has just the lone SP branchline, whereas Portland, Tacoma, and Seattle offer no less than two major rail carriers each, with fast, direct transcontinental connections.

In recent years, Southern Pacific has upgraded its trestles along the route in anticipation of possible unit-train coal traffic. The coal would be exported overseas from a terminal at Coos Bay to countries in the Pacific Rim. This would represent a tremendous economic boon to both the railroad and Coos County. As of 1993, however, the proposed coal export facility has not become a reality—partly because depressed prices in the oil market have worked

to reduce current demand for coal. And it remains unclear whether Coos Bay would be selected as a shipment point for such an operation anyway.

Unfortunately, a new nickel-ore importing facility in Coos Bay is using trucks to move raw materials to a smelter at Riddle, and thus is not utilizing the railroad. This is disappointing, as Riddle is located on SP's nearby Siskiyou Line, and bulk materials such as ore are an ideal commodity for railroads to haul.

On the positive side, a Louisiana firm, Hall-Buck Marine, Inc., has invested about $3 million in a bulk cargo shipping terminal on the Coos Bay waterfront that does rely on the railroad. In January 1993, Hall-Buck began moving carloads of copper concentrate from Kennecott mines in Utah, and stockpiling it in Coos Bay for overseas shipment. Exports are projected to total as much as 400,000 tons annually.

Above—On March 26, 1991, the Dawson Local, powered by "Kodachrome" SD9 #4363, rumbles southbound on the West Side Branch near Greenberry on its way to serve the Hull-Oakes Lumber Company sawmill at Dawson. In the background is snow-capped Marys Peak, the highest point—4,097 feet—in the Coast Range mountains.

Left—Southern Pacific SD9 #4364 and bay-window caboose #1840 rest in Corvallis Yard, covered by a blanket of snow, February 1990.

Left—LP&N Alco S2 #111 switches at Gardiner Junction, July 27, 1993. Some of Oregon's famous weather hides the trees in the background.

Above—Port of Tillamook Bay SD9 #4381 is pulling center-beam lumber cars and grain hoppers through Wilkesboro on December 16, 1988. Mt. Hood is visible in the distance.

Below—On June 19, 1990, the Coos Bay Hauler, led by SD9s #4424, #4396, and #4423 along with GP9 #3840, is passing over the Siuslaw River on the Cushman Drawbridge. A tattered boat shelter in the foreground shows off a bit of the Cushman "marina"—all part of Oregon's landscape.

Left—*The Dawson Local heads north on the West Side Branch near Corvallis, October 1990.*

Above—*LP&N Alco S2 #111 crosses the Smith River trestle near Gardiner, July 27, 1993.*

Right—*A POTB SD9-powered local nears North Plains in December 1988, on its way to interchange cars with Burlington Northern. Two cars will be left for BN and a long cut of flats carried off by the POTB. The train is running over BN's Vernonia Branch track, courtesy of an agreement between the two carriers in early 1988. Before this deal was cut, BN crews operated into Banks, 6.3 miles west of North Plains (formerly Spokane, Portland & Seattle trackage).*

Above left—Bound for Coos Bay on May 20, 1988, Cotton Belt GP40-2 #7967 leads the Coos Bay Hauler across the Cushman Drawbridge and over the blue richness of Oregon's Siuslaw River.

Below left—SP SD9 #4431 leads the Dawson Local south on the West Side Branch through Greenberry in February 1988. The pair of empty woodchip cars are bound for the sawmill at Dawson. The muddy field hints at the heavy rains the Willamette Valley receives during the winter months.

Above right—In December 1988, a Tillamook-bound Port of Tillamook Bay freight leads a cut of 11 cars across a trestle near Cochran—the summit in the line's crossing of the Coast Range mountains.

Below right—Cook, after a dusting of snow in February 1989. This lonely station is Southern Pacific's junction for the Tillamook Branch and Newberg Branch. To the left, the track heads southwest to Newberg and McMinnville. To the right, the line curves northwest to Tigard, Hillsboro, and Tillamook. Along with the service to Tillamook, the signal towers did not last; they were taken down in 1990 in favor of Direct Traffic Control blocks.

Above—SP's Tillamook Branch still sees substantial traffic on a daily basis, although much of it is coming off the nearby Newberg Branch. Here, the Newberg Turn, with SP SD9 #4353 and four other SD9s in charge of a long string of boxcars, passes through a rock cut near Lake Grove on the Tillamook Branch in June 1989. The train is returning from the Smurfit Corporation's paper mill in Newberg.

Left—Overgrown right-of-way west of Banks—remains of Spokane, Portland & Seattle's Vernonia Branch trackage.

There has also been talk now and then about a wood-chip export facility to be served by unit trains operating from Dillard on the Siskiyou Line, but this idea remains in limbo.

Still, even without these projected operations, movement on the line remains significant. Major lumber mills thrive at Coquille, North Bend, Cordes, Gardiner, Mapleton, and Vaughn, and a number of smaller facilities dot the timber-rich route. The companies operating trackside mills are pacesetters in Northwest lumbering: Weyerhaeuser. Willamette Industries. Georgia-Pacific. International Paper.

There also is a bit of liquefied petroleum gas traffic on the Coos Bay Line, plus inbound carloads of beer (one sharp reload operator in Coos Bay, Thomas & Sons, brings in boxcar shipments of beer on one spur track while loading flats with outbound lumber from off-line mills on another). Occasionally, there are hopper loads of outbound sand from the Coos Sand Company. But generally, lumber is the dominant commodity.

In recent years, the Coos Bay Hauler has operated with an alternating schedule that had a crew going on duty every morning around 6 a.m. in either Eugene or Coos Bay. Every other day, the Hauler would leave the classification yard in Eugene and run through to Coos Bay, stopping along the way as necessary to set out and pick up cars. The train generally reached its destination by late afternoon. After at least eight hours off, during which time a yard switching crew prepared an outbound train, the road crew returned to the Coos Bay depot. From Coos Bay Yard they would take eastbound (west by timetable) cars back to Eugene. The next day, the procedure was repeated as a freight train left Eugene for Coos Bay.

But train frequency on SP's Coos Bay Branch has increased. As of June 2, 1991, SP began running the Coos Bay Hauler six times a week instead of three times a week. Two different crews each make three round trips per week. One crew operates trains on Monday-Wednesday-Friday, while the other crew works Tuesday-Thursday-Saturday. The 4,520-ft. siding at Wendson—roughly halfway between Coos Bay and Eugene—is where eastbound and westbound trains plan to meet. Until the adoption of this new schedule, Wendson had been used only to store empty boxcars and flatcars. This doubling of through

SP's Cushman Turn races through Vaughn, at dusk on May 23, 1988.

service is largely a result of new export traffic being brought to the Port of Coos Bay for transport overseas. For instance, finished lumber for export is sometimes being routed to Coos Bay from a Roseburg Forest Products Company mill at Dillard on the Siskiyou Line.

Thirty miles north of Coos Bay, SP interchanges traffic with the Longview, Portland & Northern Railway. Seven days a week, the LP&N shuttles freight cars over the shortline's humble 3.5 miles of 90-lb. rail between Gardiner and its connection with the Coos Bay Branch at Gardiner Junction. At one time the LP&N—incorporated in 1922—controlled *four* Northwest shortlines, and a total of 72 miles of track. From its headquarters in Longview, Washington, the LP&N operated these lines:

- Chelatchie to Rye, Washington—30 miles. This track is now operated as the Lewis & Clark Railway. Connection: BN (ex-NP).
- Longview Junction to Ryderwood, Washington—30 miles. Abandoned in 1953.
- Gardiner to Gardiner Junction—3.5 miles. Connection: SP.
- Grand Ronde to Willamina, Oregon—8 miles. Sold to Willamina & Grand Ronde Railway in 1980. Connection: SP.

Longview, Portland & Northern Railway
Locomotive Roster

LPN #111 "Thomas Kopriva," Alco S2 (built 1949)
LPN #130 "Dale W. Zbaeren," EMD SW1500 (built 1969)

Longview, Portland & Northern Railway
Recent Carload Totals

1986	5,452
1987	5,760
1988	5,214
1989	4,920
1990	4,219
1991	4,009
1992	3,857

The Longview, Portland & Northern of the 1990s consists of only the Gardiner to Gardiner Junction segment. It was constructed in 1952 to provide an outlet for products from International Paper's mammoth mill at Gardiner. In fact, the LP&N is owned by International Paper Company, of Purchase, New York.

The Gardiner mill employs about 300 people and runs seven days a week. The shortline usually takes care of its transfer operations to Gardiner Junction early in the morning, and it is not unusual to see one of the LP&N's orange switchers—an Alco S2 or an EMD SW1500—hauling 20 or more loaded cars to the junction. Even some export paper—linerboard—is handed off to SP at Gardiner Junction for the short haul to Coos Bay. Linerboard is shipped out of Coos Bay to markets in China and Australia.

The Longview, Portland & Northern feeder provides SP with more loads than any single shipper on the branch (see chart above) and it probably deserves a place in a railroad customers' Hall of Fame somewhere. According to Basil Wheeler, IP's shipping manager at Gardiner, about 80 percent of shipments out of the facility go by railroad; only 20 percent by truck.

Besides through freights, SP has two local trains—the Coquille Local and the Cushman Turn—serving the branch. The Cushman Turn operates out of Eugene as far as Cushman and back, three times a week (round trip distance, 134 miles), switching at lumber mills along the way. The Coquille Local, on the other hand, goes on duty at 9 a.m. in Coos Bay daily except Sunday, and works in both directions out of Coos Bay Yard. This train serves customers at Coos Bay, North Bend, and Cordes, and runs south 17 miles to "end of branch" in Coquille.

Unfortunately, the Georgia-Pacific Corporation has closed two mills in Coquille in recent years. This action might doom the southern extension of the line, as the mills represented the primary shippers

Coos Bay Hauler near Gardiner Junction, July 26, 1993.

south of Coos Bay. GP's plywood mill in Coquille was Oregon's oldest, having been built in 1936, and was purchased by GP in 1956. In the wake of this action, a Roseburg Forest Products Company plywood mill about two miles north of the abandoned GP facilities in Coquille will be the only significant shipper remaining on the line past Coos Bay.

Until the early 1980s, SP trains operated another nine miles south of Coquille, to Myrtle Point. This trackage was out of service for several years, and for a

short time was offered for sale. But there were no buyers, and the short segment was finally abandoned in 1986.

At one time, a logging railroad—built by Smith-Powers Logging Company and later owned by Coos Bay Lumber Company—extended another 20 miles southeast from Myrtle Point, to a station called Powers. Trains served coal mines and timber operations in the Powers area, and SP was granted trackage rights over Coos Bay Lumber's rails to reach the

Above—*The Coos Bay Hauler switches the LP&N connection at Gardiner Junction, May 1988.*

Right—*Georgia-Pacific owned Coos Bay Lumber Company #11, a 2-8-2, is taking on water at Powers, August 14, 1964.*

Photo: Jack Holst, Collection of Pacific Northwest Chapter—National Railroad Historical Society.

Coos Bay Lumber Company #1202 at the McCormac log dump, October 10, 1954.
The large air tanks were applied for use on log trains from Powers to Coos Bay.
Jacks Photo Service, Collection of Tom Dill.

end of the line. The extension to Powers was abandoned in the early 1970s.

With the exception of signal towers controlling passage over the Reedsport and Coos Bay drawspans, there are no block signals on the route. Train movements are coordinated by direct traffic control blocks and radio-telephone communication between train crews and SP Western Region dispatchers.

The origins of the Coos Bay Branch took shape a century ago. Between 1890 and 1893, a line was constructed by the Coos Bay, Roseburg & Eastern Railroad & Navigation Company, linking Marshfield (the name for Coos Bay until an election changed it to Coos Bay in the 1940s) and Myrtle Point. At that time, it was not Eugene but Roseburg that was projected as the terminal from which a connection would be built to link Oregon's central coast with the Oregon & California mainline. For various reasons, this endeavor was never carried through.

Instead, track was laid west from Eugene by the Willamette Pacific Railroad, starting in 1913. It reached Gardiner, on the northern bank of the Umpqua River, in April 1916. From the other direction, track was being laid between Marshfield and Reedsport, on the opposite side of the Umpqua. The project was finally completed in August 1916, when a bridge spanning the river was put in place, thus officially opening the Coos Bay Line in its entirety. Meanwhile, in 1915, Southern Pacific formally purchased both the Willamette Pacific and the Coos Bay, Roseburg & Eastern, thereby acquiring ownership of what has become known as the Coos Bay Branch. They've operated it faithfully ever since.

The Coos Bay Branch is one of only a few branchlines in the state considered "Secure" by the Oregon Public Utility Commission; that is, facing no apparent threat of abandonment. But there is one serious concern in an otherwise rosy picture of the

Above—SP's Cushman Turn crosses BN's Oregon Electric Branch in Eugene.

Left—A rare sight on SP's Oregon branchlines—a signal tower protects the Umpqua River drawbridge at Reedsport, on the Coos Bay Branch.

Right—SP SD9 #4436 leads the Coos Bay Hauler into Gardiner Junction. The train is Coos Bay-bound, but first will interchange cars here with the LP&N.

Coos Bay Branch (SP)
Direct Traffic Control Blocks

Veneta Block .... West MP 652.0; East MP 664.0
Noti Block .... West MP 664.0; East MP 670.0
Richardson Block .... West MP 670.0; East MP 685.3
Tide Block .... West MP 685.3; East MP 700.0
Mapleton Block .... West MP 700.0; East MP 706.0
Wendson Block .... West MP 706.0; East MP 715.5
Canary Block .... West MP 715.5; East MP 722.0
Kroll Block .... West MP 722.0; East MP 737.2
Reedsport Block .... West MP 737.2; East MP 741.1
Lakeside Block .... West MP 741.1; East MP 752.5
Hauser Block .... West MP 752.5; East MP 762.0

route's future. Twice during 1987, again in 1989, and yet again in 1992, barges being towed by Sause Brothers Ocean Towing Company tugboats have collided with the swingspan of the drawbridge at North Bend, causing serious damage and taking the bridge out of service for days at a time. Although the railroad filed suit against the owners of the barge company to recover expenses—the parties settled out of court for an undisclosed sum—there was a strong hint from SP officials that after several accidents, their patience was wearing thin. In the event of another serious incident, they might choose not to repair the bridge again, thereby effectively closing some 23 miles of track. This would force several Coos Bay and Coquille businesses to haul their products to a reload

site north of the railroad bridge. Recent Oregon PUC figures indicate there are as many as 10 shippers located south of the bridge, and together they have accounted for approximately 2,300 carloads per year.

In another development, the venerable SP depot in Coos Bay, built decades ago, was torn down in July 1990 to make way for an extensive rebuilding of Highway 101 across town. The new four-lane route also forced the removal of some tracks from Coos Bay Yard. A new station, paid for by the city, was constructed in the vicinity.

New owner Denver & Rio Grande Western appears to remain interested in the potential that the Port of Coos Bay holds. Even before the 1988 acquisition of SP was finalized, D&RGW donated $10,000

for a feasibility study detailing ways Coos Bay could actively compete for about 2 million tons of cargo currently going north to Seattle and Tacoma. The Port of Coos Bay could become a much more important West Coast terminal if D&RGW's aspirations pay off.

In addition, D&RGW's entry makes it more likely that a new coal export terminal will be located in Coos Bay. Instead of handing coal traffic over to the UP in Utah for movement westward, as is currently done, the D&RGW can logically be expected to make a strong effort to hold on to that lucrative traffic. Since the D&RGW now holds title to a good Pacific Ocean port at Coos Bay, a number of interesting changes may be looming on the horizon.

Above—SSW GP40-2s #7967 and #7964 escort SP slug #1613 and two SD9s—
#4409 and #4410—at Cordes on the Coos Bay Branch, May 20, 1988.

Above right—The Coos Bay Hauler working in Cordes, just a few miles from its
final destination: Coos Bay Yard.

Below right—On October 10, 1988, the Coos Bay Hauler stops to leave a boxcar
at the Cushman spur.

CHAPTER 3

EXPANSION FROM TILLAMOOK BAY

*Port of Tillamook Bay Railroad and Southern Pacific's Tillamook Branch,
with Burlington Northern connecting lines
Vernonia Branch and Forest Grove Branch*

The Port of Tillamook Bay Railroad is a textbook shortline. For decades, the carrier could claim only 3.4 miles of track as its own. But in the 1980s, the POTB's operations stretched many dozens of miles beyond its home in Tillamook—first to Batterson, and later as far as Hillsboro and North Plains.

Tillamook is a quiet town on the Oregon coast with a population of approximately 4,000. Its namesake railroad is owned by the Port of Tillamook Bay, a modest jurisdiction with no active water-related facilities. Rather, the port authority owns and operates an airport, an industrial park, and the railroad.

For more than 70 years, the line from Tillamook to Batterson and Hillsboro—officially known as the Tillamook Branch—was in the hands of Southern Pacific. In fact, one station on the line—Salmonberry—enjoyed the distinction of being the northernmost point on the entire SP system. But that's history now.

It was perhaps inevitable that Southern Pacific would move to delete the 115-mile Tillamook Branch from its operations. The line is mountain-rugged, with steep gradients (as much as 3.2 percent in places), numerous tunnels, and tight, 17-degree curves highlighting a long and winding route through the Coast Range. Indeed, a general rule of thumb concerning SP's operations on the branch was that one locomotive was required for every five freight cars being pulled.

It added up to being expensive railroading—

uneconomical enough for SP to take two drastic steps. To begin with, in September 1985, the carrier placed the portion of the line west of Hillsboro into "Category 1": subject to abandonment within three years. Then in January 1986, SP slapped a $645 per car surcharge onto shipments moving over the line, a dramatic indication that it wanted out. In the face of SP's abandonment efforts, and believing the line merited preservation, the Port of Tillamook Bay stepped in.

Prior to 1983, the POTB was an all-but-invisible shortline carrier that existed almost exclusively to serve Louisiana-Pacific's massive sawmill and plywood facility in the Tillamook Industrial Park. The 1983 closure of Louisiana-Pacific's Tillamook complex—at that time it was Tillamook County's largest employer—threatened not only the POTB, but the future of the Tillamook Branch itself. Economic survival for the city and its tiny railroad demanded an aggressive stance.

With the industrial park and the SP interchange in Tillamook as its base, the Port of Tillamook Bay moved to widen its reach. First, a January 1983 trackage rights agreement with SP allowed the smaller railroad to operate from Tillamook to Batterson, a distance of 30.7 miles. Three years later, in May 1986, another trackage rights agreement was finalized, permitting the carrier to work the SP branchline as far east as Mahan, 90 miles from the railroad's Tillamook home. (Mahan is on the outskirts of Hillsboro, 1.6 miles west of the SP depot.) Next, on December 17, 1986, SP permanently vacated the trackage from Tillamook to Hillsboro.

Outright purchase of the property remained a key objective of the Port's managers, and their patience

---

SP's Tillamook Branch at Cochran in 1976. A Portland-bound Tillamook Hauler is carrying a long cut of woodchip cars from the Louisiana-Pacific mill at Tillamook.

Tillamook Branch (SP)
Stations

Port of Tillamook Bay SD9 #4368 sits in the Tillamook Industrial Park, June 1991. This is one of three ex-SP units on the initial POTB roster.

was rewarded on February 1, 1990. On that day—for $2.9 million—Southern Pacific deeded its track between Tillamook and Schefflin (Schefflin is 5.2 miles northwest of Hillsboro) to the Port of Tillamook Bay Railroad. The POTB continues to hold operating rights all the way to Mahan, where it interchanges traffic with SP.

The remainder of Southern Pacific's Tillamook Branch heads east from Hillsboro to Willsburg Junction, where the branch begins and where it connects with SP's Valley Line. This 24-mile portion of the Tillamook Branch is a relatively busy property, as it serves a number of diverse shippers in industrial parks in Milwaukie, Lake Oswego, Tigard, Beaverton, and Hillsboro.

The Tillamook Branch is SP's only direct rail link between Brooklyn Yard in Portland and a fistful of important outlying stations to the west, including Newberg, McMinnville, Seghers, Willamina, and Hillsboro. Traffic off the Newberg Branch, West Side-Seghers Branch, and Willamina Branch all funnels onto the Tillamook Branch at Cook, a key junction and gateway to the Valley Line and Portland. At Cook, the Newberg and Tillamook branchlines converge, with the line to Newberg and McMinnville curving southwest, and the line to Hillsboro and Tillamook bending toward the northwest.

Southern Pacific moves several trains over the Cook-Willsburg Junction segment (7.3 miles) of the Tillamook Branch every day. Trains moving out of Brooklyn Yard for points west include the Newberg Turn, between Brooklyn and Newberg, and the Whiteson Turn, between Brooklyn and McMinnville. Both trains are active six days per week, and both are powered by multiple SD9s—usually four or five units each. And both trains switch onto the Newberg Branch at Cook.

In addition, the Brooklyn-based Clackamas Switcher works westward through Lake Oswego and Cook to Tigard, where it interchanges cars with a local out of Hillsboro. Along the way, the Clackamas Switcher serves the James River Corporation's woodchip dump at Lake Oswego. Further to the west, SP's Hillsboro Local—also known as the Hillsboro Roustabout—works Monday through Friday on the Tillamook Branch between Hillsboro and Cook, where it interchanges with the Clackamas Switcher.

Lumber is the lifeblood for a number of railroads, and this is certainly true of the Port of Tillamook Bay. Here, SD9 #4368 heads straight into the sun as it nears Hillsboro on a cold winter morning. In tow are four flats of lumber for interchange with SP at Mahan, 1.6 miles west of Hillsboro.

By taking over operation of the 90-mile segment between Hillsboro and Tillamook, the Port of Tillamook Bay has in a sense brought the history of the trackage full circle. This mileage represents the original route of the Pacific Railway & Navigation Company and the POTB is heir to that historic line. The connection to Tillamook was built by the Pacific Railway & Navigation Company early in the 20th century, with roadbed construction beginning at both ends—Hillsboro and Tillamook—in 1906. The route was intended to connect Tillamook with the Willamette Valley, thereby opening the coast's rich timberlands to commerce and its popular beach resorts to tourists. The first train came through from Portland to Tillamook in October 1911. In 1915, however, PR&N sold the line to SP.

At Tillamook in 1942, the U.S. Navy built and began operating a short rail extension from the end of the SP line to a blimp base—Naval Air Station Tillamook—located south of town. During World War II, eight Navy "K-series" blimps based in Tillamook patrolled coastal waters, searching for Japanese submarines. After the war, the Navy eventually pulled out of Tillamook and the port district stepped in during the 1950s—buying the land and converting it into an industrial park. The railway was included in the purchase, and thus the Port of Tillamook Bay Railroad was born.

In recent years, the state of Oregon has assisted the growing shortline with some very sorely needed rehabilitation monies. Financial grants, first through Local Rail Service Assistance (a federal program

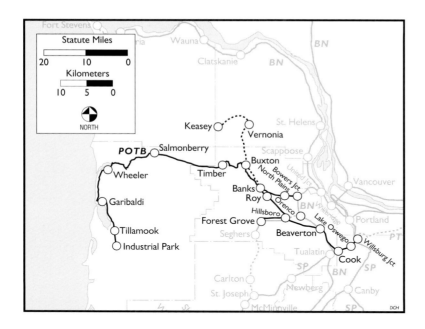

Port of Tillamook Bay Railroad and Southern Pacific's Tillamook Branch,
with Burlington Northern connecting lines Vernonia Branch and Forest Grove Branch

administered by the Department of Transportation)
and later through state lottery revenues, totaled almost $500,000 over an eight-year period. And after
severe flooding in Tillamook County in January 1990
washed out sections of the rail line to Hillsboro,
$600,000 in emergency repair funding was granted.
The line reopened on March 13, 1990. In addition to
these projects, the POTB's original 3.4 miles of road-
way has been rebuilt with 75-lb. and 90-lb. rail, and
bedded with sand and pit run ballast. Top speed over
this short segment is 10 mph.

The expanded POTB's new mileage benefited
from SP's bigger maintenance-of-way budgets.
Fortunately for the Port of Tillamook Bay, SP track
crews kept the Tillamook Branch in fairly good shape
over the years—no casual feat for mountain trackage
requiring almost constant attention. Built and maintained with a substantially higher capability than the
POTB's original track, most of the line is in Class 2
condition, with freight trains permitted to move at 20
mph. The steel rail ranges from 80-lb. track between
Tillamook and Batterson, to 132-lb. rail in large sections from Batterson to Schefflin. Ties overall are fair

to good, with crushed rock used as ballast along most
of the right-of-way.

Despite the devastating economic effects of terri-
ble forest fires in the 1930s (the "Tillamook Burn"
consumed over 240,000 acres of prime timber),
replanting in the area has been amazingly successful.
Trees in what is now the 364,000-acre Tillamook
State Forest—spreading across much of Tillamook
and Washington counties—are once again approach-
ing harvest size. The Port of Tillamook Bay is
positioned to take advantage of this. Within 15 years,
the area's forest products industry could be booming,
and this would contribute a "considerable" increase
in carloadings on the line, according to an Oregon
Public Utility Commission study.

Forest products have always been the prime
commodity moving over the branch. Log trains were
once an everyday sight, and for many years sidings
along the route were jammed with gondolas and flatcars being loaded with logs for transfer to Willamette
Valley sawmills. Even after the Tillamook Burn,
lucrative salvage operations continued for years.

Southern Pacific handled about 7,000 cars on the

Hillsboro-Tillamook portion of the branchline in 1974, a healthy level of business. But just 10 years later that number had plummeted to 2,394, owing in large part to the closure of the Louisiana-Pacific plant, which had been good for nearly 50 carloads of lumber weekly. Accordingly, train service fell precipitously. In 1978, frequency was steady at six days per week, but by 1985 freights came over the scenic line only once or twice a week. As late as June of 1985, the Oregon Department of Transportation had this to say regarding the status of the Port of Tillamook Bay Railroad:

> In limbo. Likely to be abandoned, even if a very substantial rail service user can be found, since Southern Pacific's Tillamook Branch is also a likely abandonment candidate and provides only connection to rail system.

In the early 1990s, all movements of POTB trains over the Coast Range are flexible, subject to change depending on connecting traffic and shipper needs. Banks and Hillsboro have become the eastern bases of operations, with Tillamook serving as the western base. Twice a week, on Wednesdays and Saturdays, one train leaves Mahan (MP 766.4) while another departs Tillamook (MP 855.8). The trains meet at Enright (MP 811.0) to exchange cars, then return to where they originated to tie up. Enright is almost precisely halfway between the two stations. Depending upon the availability of locomotives, however, sometimes a crew will take a train west to Tillamook on Wednesdays and Saturdays, and haul eastbound cars back to Hillsboro the following day.

The POTB's two-member crews usually go on duty early in the morning. As a result, most of the railroad's work takes place in daylight. Thus, twice a week, a train of loaded lumber cars and empty grain hoppers can be seen gliding out of Tillamook, winding along the craggy coastline and through a series of quaint bay-front communities before cutting hard

Cochran—A once-busy timber town on the Southern Pacific's Tillamook Branch, circa 1920.

Photo: Guy L. Dunscomb, Collection of Tom Dill.

*A Tillamook-bound freight rolls through Twin Rocks in December 1988. Twin Rocks,
one of many resort towns POTB train crews encounter, is seen here near sunset.*

inland at Wheeler. From there, the freight continues over the Coast Range to Mahan, with tall trestles and numerous tunnels lining the route. The rigorous 90-mile journey requires approximately six hours.

Along the way, the train passes through what were once major railroad stations at Timber and Cochran. At 1,824 feet, Cochran is the summit of the Tillamook Branch, and once was an important interchange point for the Cochran & Southern Railroad, a logging road. The station at Timber, in addition to being a base for helper engines, was the crew-change point for Tillamook Branch trains. The Timber roundhouse, depot, water tower, and crew hotel were kept constantly busy by trains coming and going. Now, virtually all trace of the activity that once took place in Timber and Cochran has

Tillamook Branch (SP)
Direct Traffic Control Blocks

Menefee Block	West MP 743.7; East MP 741.6
Lake Oswego Block	West MP 744.9; East MP 743.7
Cook Block	West MP 748.1; East MP 744.9
Tigard Block	West MP 751.8; East MP 748.1
Reedville Block	West MP 764.2; East MP 756.9

Port of Tillamook Bay Railroad
Recent Carload Totals

1986	1,181
1987	1,088
1988	1,049
1989	1,076
1990	622
1991	1,326
1992	1,524

vanished. A long siding at Cochran is just about all that remains of either station.

Banks has replaced Timber and Cochran as one of the Port of Tillamook Bay Railroad's key stations on the eastern side of the mountains. This rural Washington County town, with about 600 residents, is home to the Banks Lumber Company—which requires switching almost daily. Banks also serves as a gateway to connections with Southern Pacific and Burlington Northern in Hillsboro and North Plains respectively.

North Plains represents the latest addition to the POTB's increasing range. Early in 1988, the shortline concluded an agreement with Burlington Northern that provides POTB with trackage rights over BN-owned track to reach North Plains, where the two railroads interchange cars. North Plains is located 6.3 miles east of Banks, on the old Spokane, Portland & Seattle Railway's Vernonia Branch. The Vernonia Branch, originally constructed for United Railways, once reached as far north as Keasey, 31 miles beyond Banks. Its route included a seven-mile stretch of side-by-side running with SP's Tillamook Branch between Buxton and Wilkesboro. Most of the Vernonia line was abandoned in the 1970s, and the track beyond Banks has been removed. (The state of Oregon recently opened a "linear park"—with a trail for horseback riding, bicycling, and hiking—along the former Vernonia Branch right-of-way between Banks and Vernonia, 21 miles.)

Vernonia Branch trackage, now owned by Burlington Northern, continues to recede. Officially, the branch begins at Bowers Junction and extends directly west to Banks via North Plains, a total of 11.2

Above—June 1991: Burlington Northern's North Plains Local switches in North Plains with leased GP38-2 #781.

Right—Banks at the end of the BN Vernonia Branch, July 1991. The Port of Tillamook Bay Railroad operates up to this point.

miles. But no BN trains have rolled into Banks since 1988, when the POTB began going to North Plains.

On Tuesdays and Thursdays, a BN crew out of Beaverton serves the POTB interchange and the remaining customer in North Plains—Van Dyke Grain Elevators, Inc., which brings in a steady stream of livestock feed and cottonseed for area dairy farmers. What's left of the Vernonia Branch is in generally poor condition, with 75-lb. rail and many decaying ties; clearly it has been neglected. Between Bowers Junction and Banks, this line is identified as "excepted" under FRA Track Safety Standards Rule 213.4. This means that the speed limit for all trains on the branch is restricted to a maximum of 10 mph.

The branchline was much more important to BN before 1988, when the Vernonia trackage was used to provide access onto BN's 5.7-mile Forest Grove Branch between Hillsboro and Forest Grove. The Burlington Northern's local trains have been going into Forest Grove three times a week in recent years, primarily with inbound tank cars of corn syrup for the Gray & Company cherry plant, or reefers of frozen fruit and vegetable products for Henningsen Cold Storage Company. BN trains had been forced to wind along a terribly indirect, convoluted routing that saw crews pick up their power at Beaverton, follow the Oregon Electric Branch to Bowers Junction (9.3 miles), and then cut onto the Vernonia Branch to get to Banks (another 11.2 miles). In Banks, BN trains switched onto SP's Tillamook Branch, then moved over 9.2 miles of SP property to reach Hillsboro. Finally, in Hillsboro, BN's local crews transferred onto the BN-owned Forest Grove Branch and proceeded another five miles to reach shippers in Forest Grove. Saving everyone involved a lot of headaches, SP and BN finally closed a deal granting BN direct access from Beaverton, at MP 755.6, to BN Junction, MP 765.5, in Hillsboro. This means that BN crews now travel about 16 miles one-way to Forest Grove, instead of 37 miles.

The Port of Tillamook Bay has negotiated to buy all of what remains of the Vernonia Branch—from Banks through North Plains to Bowers Junction—where it connects with BN's active Oregon Electric Branch. There are indications lately, however, that BN may want to keep the route intact.

Another change took place in the 1980s, when

Port of Tillamook Bay Railroad
Locomotive Roster (January 1993)

POTB #4368, EMD SD9E (ex-SP, built 1955)
POTB #4381, EMD SD9E (ex-SP, built 1955)
POTB #4414, EMD SD9E (ex-SP, built 1956)
POTB #110, GE 80T Switcher (built 1943; out of service)
POTB #111, GE 80T Switcher (built 1943; out of service)

the city planners of Beaverton came up with millions of dollars to reroute BN's Oregon Electric line away from the city's hopelessly congested business district. As a result, all BN through trains now share SP's Tillamook Branch rails for about five miles, between Greton, MP 751.9 (near Tigard), and St. Marys, MP 756.9 (near Beaverton).

Due to the Port of Tillamook Bay Railroad's move onto BN property and its expansion along SP's Tillamook Branch, the POTB has gone from serving just 3.4 miles to nearly 100 miles since 1983. Not bad for a carrier being measured for a coffin! To power its trains, the POTB owns three road locomotives, all former SP SD9s. Two old GE 80-ton center-cab switchers sitting in the POTB's industrial park are no longer used, and the Port owns no cabooses.

There are a handful of steady shippers on the branch. Tillamook Lumber Company (owned by Hampton Industries) in Tillamook, and Banks Lumber Company in Banks have been the line's primary forest products shippers; and the Tillamook County Creamery Association, producer of the popular Tillamook cheeses, brings in carloads of grain to feed its herds of dairy cows in Tillamook. The creamery has committed to hauling almost all of its inbound feed by rail, and is building a new seven-car unloading facility in the port's industrial park to handle increased shipments. A "dramatic jump" of inbound carloads of grain is expected after the new site's mid-1994 opening, according to Ed Immel, a rail planner for the Oregon Department of Transportation. Current capacity is two cars, at a loading dock across Highway 101. Switching crews are required to move grain cars across a four-lane highway in downtown Tillamook to get to the present location—an obvious headache.

There is growing potential for hauling woodchips

July 27, 1990: recognizing the importance of upkeep, the Port of Tillamook Bay Railroad has brought in a couple of flatcar loads of new ties for the maintenance crew. Two of the road's SD9s, #4414 and #4368, rest after delivering this essential cargo to the Port's industrial park, a few months after the POTB bought most of the Tillamook Branch from Southern Pacific.

from the Hampton Industries facility that has located in Tillamook. Hampton owns a sizable operation that currently delivers woodchips—by truck—to a paper mill at Wauna, located on the Columbia River along BN's Astoria Line. The Hampton plant's capacity could be as much as 8 to 10 carloads of chips per day—translating into a substantial increase in tonnage for the carrier. But unless, and until, such an agreement is struck, the Hampton facility in Tillamook will continue to see trucks driven over spur tracks to load up with chips from a spout designed to fill railroad cars. Word is that SP did not give its woodchip traffic expedited delivery, and the chips aged, making them less desirable for use in making paper. The Port of Tillamook Bay appears to be paying for SP's neglect of this commodity.

The new WTD Industries lumber mill in the Tillamook industrial park, which promised to move up to eight boxcar loads over the line every day, has been unable to secure a reliable supply of logs to put the mill into full operation. Some boxcars are being hauled, however, and this is another success on the line's slow return to viability.

In a somewhat contentious development, John Hampton, president of Tillamook Lumber Company, has warned Bruce Engel, president of WTD Industries that, in effect, "This town isn't big enough for both of us." Hampton contends there won't be enough logs to feed two Tillamook mills. Despite the aggressive rivalry for logs, it seems the WTD mill may be more likely to survive in the long run, because it is more modern and efficient, and has been designed to process smaller logs.

In addition, a new lumber mill—Garibaldi Hardwood Company—opened in Garibaldi in 1990. The company built a spur into its facility to move carloads of wood products. This is another important customer, and should help to solidify the POTB's revenue base.

Two huge World War II-era blimp hangars in the port's industrial park—Hangar A and Hangar B—enabled the Port of Tillamook Bay to attract some unique tenants over the years. The Navy built these hangars in an immense size, with each measuring 1,072 feet long, 296 feet wide, and 170 feet high (they were reported to be the world's largest wooden structures by the *Guinness Book of World Records*). From 1952 to 1973, Hangar A contained a Diamond B Lumber plywood mill; Hangar B housed a sawmill. (Diamond B Lumber was purchased by Louisiana-Pacific, which operated in Tillamook until 1983.)

The awesome structures also provided an opportunity to attract a new railroad-related firm: namely, the Tillamook Railcar Repair Company, which was superseded by Oregon Coastline Express, Inc. (d.b.a. Bob Steele & Associates, Inc.). These companies needed a large enclosed area, with rail access and track space to accommodate the refurbishing of passenger cars. The blimp hangars, with spur tracks and some seven and one-half acres under roof, came made-to-order. A fleet of 1955-era SP double-deck commuter cars, delivered by the POTB, provided raw stock for the transformations. Bob Steele & Associates (see chapter four) rebuilds passenger cars, adding plush seats, open observation decks, unusually high

Above—The Port of Tillamook Bay Railroad now operates two lines through Banks, where BN's Vernonia Branch connected with SP's Tillamook Branch. The Banks Lumber Company keeps the carrier busy.

Left—Spokane, Portland & Seattle's abandoned trestle at Hares Creek on the Vernonia Branch.

Photo: Jack Holst, Collection of PNWC—NRHS.

Left—SP SD9 #4373 sits at Hillsboro on the Tillamook Branch, June 1991. This station was once a busy junction; the Tillamook Branch and the West Side Branch split here.

Right—SP SD9 #4353 leads a train of boxcars, the Newberg Turn, toward Portland, June 1989. Between Willsburg Junction and Cook, the Newberg Turn travels along the Tillamook Branch.

domes, gourmet kitchens, etc., for special rail tours.

Unfortunately, a fire in August 1992 destroyed one of the famous hangars. Hangar A had been filled with hay scheduled to be shipped to Japan when flames reduced the mammoth structure to rubble. Hangar B remained undamaged. Bob Steele housed his operation in Hangar A, but luckily, none of his equipment was inside at the time of the conflagration.

The Tillamook route, due in good measure to its scenic setting (Ed Austin and Tom Dill, authors of the excellent book *The Southern Pacific in Oregon*, refer to the branchline as "the most spectacular in Oregon"), has attracted several entrepreneurs to take a hard, imaginative look at the line's tourism potential. For years, there have been ideas afoot to run tourist excursion trains out of Tillamook during the summer season. One such plan became reality in May 1989, as Bob Steele's Oregon Coastline Express excursion trains began rolling from Tillamook to Wheeler, a 22-mile trip one way—much of it directly along the coastline. The operation had a relatively successful couple of years before being halted in 1991. There has also been talk of a dinner train operating between Hillsboro and Tillamook (see chapter four).

All indications are that the Denver & Rio Grande Western Railroad's announced commitment to revitalize SP rail service will have a positive impact on the Port of Tillamook Bay. In fact, many Oregon officials have publicly expressed the belief that the Rio Grande's arrival is one of the best things that could have happened to transportation-dependent businesses throughout Oregon's SP network.

Furthermore, in May 1991, the Port of Tillamook Bay hired a private firm—Rail West—to manage operations on the railroad. Owned by David and Mike Root, the same team that owns the Willamette Valley Railroad and the Willamina & Grand Ronde Railway (see chapter seven), Rail West's experience in all facets of the railroad industry was expected to improve the line's fortunes.

With business beginning to increase on this mountainous line, maintenance-of-way teams are at work to improve the roadbed. Track speeds may rise to 40 mph from the current 20 mph after more ties (including some steel ones) and heavier rail are put into place. Moreover, the Willamette Valley Railroad's ex-SP GP9, long in storage at Independence, is slated for repair. After this is completed, it may be assigned to duty on the Port of Tillamook Bay Railroad.

A challenging period of transition has produced impressive growth for the POTB, leaving the carrier with a chance to prosper. With its improved management, and the promise of extra revenue from tourist train operations, the future for the line is no longer as grim as it seemed just a few years ago.

Left above—SP SD9s #4363 and #4323, power for the Hillsboro Roustabout, idle in the Hillsboro yard before heading back to Portland, July 25, 1990.

Left—Port of Tillamook Bay SD9 #4381, ready for work in Hillsboro.

Above—SP Baldwin S-10 #1867 rests beside Portland's Brooklyn Yard roundhouse in August 1968, after building the Tillamook Hauler.
Photo: Jack Holst, Collection of PNWC—NRHS.

Right—A Port of Tillamook Bay center-cab switcher sits in the Tillamook Industrial Park in 1969.
Photo: Walt Grande.

Below—BN's North Plains Local, with GP38-2 #781 on the point, rounds a bend outside of North Plains on the Vernonia Branch, June 20, 1991. The crew is headed home to Beaverton.

Above—An Oregon Coastline Express excursion train, pulled by OCE #702, an Alco C415, discharges sightseers on the "Rock Coast Route," summer 1990.
Collection of Oregon Coastline Express.

Left—Inside "Banks," the finely crafted bar car on the Spirit of Oregon dinner train.
Photo: Charlie Kloppenburg.

CHAPTER 4

HEAVY INDUSTRY AND TOURISM: TILLAMOOK'S FINE MIX

Passenger car renovations and Oregon Coastline Express excursion trains

On May 26, 1989, the Oregon Coastline Express began operating daily excursion trains between Tillamook and Wheeler, a distance of 22 miles, with stops along the way in Garibaldi and Rockaway Beach. The colorful trains, with two elegant passenger cars named *Hebo* and *Neah-Kah-Nie*, were a symbol of the importance of tourism to the area. For two summers, crowds could be seen boarding at the renovated Tillamook depot for a spectacular four-hour, round-trip journey along what was being called Oregon's "Rock Coast Route."

There had been talk in Tillamook County for years about the potential economic value of operating a tour train along the Oregon shoreline from Tillamook to Wheeler. Over most of the route, the tracks are located close to the shoreline and west of Highway 101. Especially with this selling point, a passenger train's ability to lure more tourists to the area seemed undeniable, and communities along the coast depend on tourism. It appeared to be a project just waiting to be realized; for someone to step forward to cement some kind of deal. But other than talk about what a good idea a tour train would be, nothing happened.

That rankled Bob Steele. He's not one for a lot of aimless talk, nor for hearing that something can't be done.

"The governor promotes tourism, and tourism is about all Oregon's got left," Steele says, citing the difficulties facing so many Northwest lumber mills. "If we'd been stopped from running our train, I'd have pulled the engine and cars out to the depot and called the biggest press conference this county's ever seen, and let someone explain why we can't operate this beautiful train."

Steele and his wife Vickie are co-owners of Oregon Coastline Express, Inc., and founders of the excursion trains. They have not been afraid to gamble on success. Start-up costs for the excursion train project, which they pushed through seemingly overnight, resulted in almost $80,000 in losses in 1990, and the enterprise required $10 million worth of liability insurance. For locomotive power, the Steeles purchased three engines from Weyerhaeuser's Columbia & Cowlitz Railway, based in Longview, Washington. The three units, two Alco C415s and a Morrison-Knudsen slug (rebuilt from an Alco S6), cost a total of $235,000. It's a lot of money—but the Steeles are patient enough to take the long view.

"We built the train," Bob says, "and we built it on spec."

The new passenger service attracted important guests in its first few months of operation. Governor Neil Goldschmidt came to town to travel the route on its inaugural run and provide some valuable "Made In Oregon" boosterism. Then in August 1989, Tillamook and the Oregon Coastline Express played host to the Oregon Mayor's Association conference, when mayors from all over the state enjoyed a ride on the train as part of their working tour. Tillamook Mayor Bob McPheeters basked in his fellow mayors' praise for days after that. And successful gubernatorial candidate Barbara Roberts visited the depot and inspected the interiors of the tour trains during a campaign appearance in Tillamook in May 1990.

After the Steeles' first excursion train became a reality, Bob immediately turned to other ideas. He wanted to hang a B-52 bomber in one of the blimp hangars, and build a caboose train to carry tourists to the hangar to see it.

A line of former commuter cars waits for renovation next to one of the ex-U.S. Navy blimp hangars at the Port of Tillamook Bay's Industrial Park in 1989.

"Maybe it's all dreams," he says. "But that's where it starts."

Thanks to the Steeles' efforts, glory days could be returning to the Tillamook Line, which once bustled with passenger trains shuttling back and forth between the Portland area and the many coastal resorts in Tillamook County. Three sections of scheduled passenger trains were not uncommon on summer weekends, until all-weather roadways made the coastline easily accessible by automobile. Southern Pacific ended regular passenger service to Tillamook in 1953.

Bob Steele, now in his 50s, was born in Nevada City, California. Somewhat surprisingly, he's never been employed by a railroad. Yet he's been a member of at least four labor unions—Ironworkers, Operating Engineers, Boilermakers, and Machinery Workers—whose crafts mesh exceedingly well with his Tillamook operation. In addition, for years he managed diesel engine sales and service facilities (marine and trucking) in Seattle, Coos Bay, and Newport.

Fortunately for economically pressed Tillamook County, Bob and Vickie settled in for the long haul. They purchased a home in Oceanside, a few miles

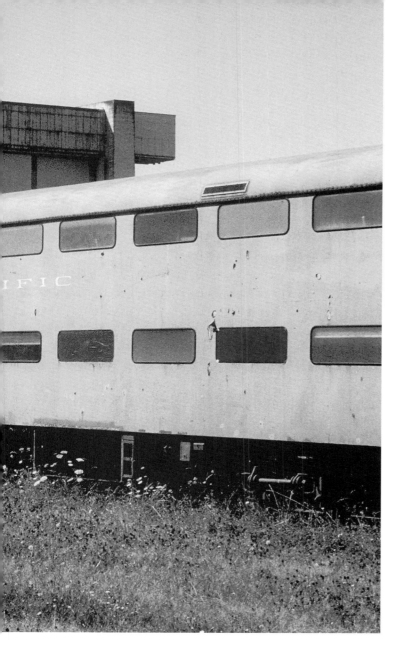

occasionally were called upon to supply motive power for the excursion train when OCE #702, the line's "flagship" locomotive, was down for repair.

Actually, the excursion trains are merely a sideline to the Steeles' bread and butter business: rehabilitating railroad passenger cars for tour lines and private owners. Doing business as Bob Steele & Associates, Inc. (BS&A), the Steeles fashioned a system that transformed $11,000 "scrap" railroad cars into plush, steel-wheeled, rolling luxury liners. The two former Southern Pacific, 1955-era, bi-level commuter cars he converted for use on his OCE trains, for example, now are valued at nearly $300,000 each.

"I don't understand why the railroads scrapped their stainless steel cars," Bob says. "A locomotive will wear out, but these cars go on forever."

The Steeles' timing seems perfect. Nationally, Amtrak ridership is climbing, and the trend is reflected in Oregon's Amtrak passenger totals. In 1987, 451,543 travelers arrived or departed on trains serving Oregon's 13 Amtrak stations. By 1992, that figure had jumped to 496,929—a 10.1 percent increase in five years. The need for improved rail passenger equipment is clear.

"Growing demand for Amtrak services nationwide

from the enormous, former U.S. Navy blimp hangar that housed their offices in the Port of Tillamook Bay Industrial Park, until the August 22, 1992, fire destroyed the building.

The freight-hauling Port of Tillamook Bay Railroad, which has jurisdiction over the route traversed by Oregon Coastline Express excursion trains, finalized purchase of the SP line between Tillamook and Hillsboro in 1990. This is an important step for the POTB, as well as for the area's economic development. It also proved to be a great convenience for Oregon Coastline Express. The POTB's locomotives

Blimps at the Tillamook Naval Air Station in 1943.
Photo: U.S. Navy, Collection of Lydia Irwin.

is outstripping our capacity to provide it," W. Graham Claytor, Jr., president of Amtrak, told a U.S. Senate subcommittee in 1989.

While Amtrak was never a direct customer, many of the cars renovated in Tillamook ended up being pulled in the consists of Amtrak trains, including the popular Los Angeles-Seattle *Coast Starlight*. This is precisely the same concept behind the tremendously successful *Midnight Sun Express* tours between Anchorage and Fairbanks, Alaska. Swank "Ultra Dome" passenger cars—refurbished by Bob Steele and Tom Rader (the founder of Tillamook Railcar Repair Company) in a joint 1987-1988 project—are now being towed behind the Alaska Railroad's daily train on the "Mount McKinley Route."

By 1989, the Steeles' company was beginning to get more orders than it was able to handle. At most, a total of 11 or 12 passenger cars could be squeezed onto the lone rail spur running through the middle of the cavernous hangar. To overcome this limitation, construction of a new 25,000 square foot facility in Tillamook, with at least two service tracks, was on the drawing board for awhile, but the plan was eventually shelved.

John Kirkwood, president of Rail Ventures, a California-based company that operates a pool of private railcars—Rail Venture cars *Bella Vista* and *Yerba Buena* were upgraded at Tillamook in 1989—sees a growing demand for first-class rail travel far beyond what Amtrak can provide. Kirkwood, who admits that his fascination with private railcars has become "an addiction," hopes to fill the bill by arranging new railroad trips for his customers.

Bob Steele & Associates provides companies such as Rail Ventures, Holland America West, and Princess Tours—pacesetters in the luxury tour business—with passenger cars filled with "cruise ship amenities," including two-level suites (a spiral staircase connects the levels), exercise rooms, hot tubs, private bars, full-length mirrors, baths and showers, VCRs, oak finishings, and fine dining. Perhaps most dramatic, passengers can go to bed in their own private sleeping dome atop the train. The end result is like traveling in a first-class hotel room, and berths can be expensive. Some "cruises" in a private railcar with an on-board chef go for as much as $3,000 per day.

"They don't look like much now," Bob admits, pointing to a line of old, decrepit commuter cars seemingly abandoned on a siding. "But when they're put together, they'll stand tall."

Loram Rail Grinding Service, a railway maintenance firm based in Hamel, Minnesota, has provided an interesting extension to the Steeles' endeavors in the passenger car market. Loram contracted with BS&A to rebuild two weather-beaten, former SP bi-level commuter cars into bunk cars for track grinding crews working primarily in Canada. Normally, a railroad laborer's bunk car wouldn't be considered a first-class accommodation. But when the finished cars rolled out of Tillamook a few weeks after the Steeles' skilled team got ahold of them, they sported shiny brass sinks, large windows, fancy light fixtures, thick carpet, birchwood framing, 14 comfortable bunks, air conditioning, a kitchen with electric range, recliners, four showers per car, and an on-board clothes washer and dryer!

Even the 15-foot-high roofs were cut off and rebuilt to 17-feet, one inch. "More headroom," explains Bob.

The Steeles' crews worked 10-hour days, four days a week, and some of the most exclusive railcars in

North America rolled out of that dusty, 1942-era blimp hangar. Expert craftsmanship was the order of the day on the rebuild line.

"We created jobs here—and we don't pay minimum wage," Bob says proudly. Many of his employees had been laid off from area lumber mills, and his pride is justifiable.

The unique combination of tourism and industry is slowly helping to boost Oregon's north coast region. With the long-envisioned excursion trains and the passenger car rehabilitation business, Bob and Vickie Steele have been able to provide a depressed local economy with the fruits of dozens of new jobs. On May 1, 1990, after taking the winter off, Oregon Coastline Express began rolling again, on tracks that had survived heavy winter storms and subsequent flooding in Tillamook County.

True to Bob's dreams, with the coming of the new season the Steeles also inaugurated a new train. In addition to the Alco C415-powered trains plowing along the "Rock Coast Route," a "Caboose Run" was added to the schedule. The "maiden voyage" of the first caboose train in Tillamook's history began at 10:30 a.m. on Tuesday, May 1, 1990, at the former SP depot in Tillamook. The caboose train went from the depot to the blimp hangars three miles south of town. Equipment for this train consisted of two renovated ex-Burlington Northern cabooses (BN #12118 and FW&D #174) pulled by a GE 65T center-cab diesel. The cabooses and locomotive were freshly painted in a BN-inspired green, white, and yellow scheme. All of the cabooses, locomotives, and passenger cars used in both trains were renovated in the Steeles' shops.

The concept behind the caboose train was simple, but unique: passengers rode in rebuilt cabooses fitted with extra-large (32" x 32") "picture windows" to put all the sights on display. The diesel locomotive pulled the cabooses right up to the doors of the blimp hangars, whereupon passengers left the train and boarded a bus that carried them inside. After a tour, passengers climbed back aboard the cabooses and were hauled back to Tillamook.

It all sounded positive. But apparently there were some "internal difficulties" with the Port of Tillamook Bay, involving labor and personality conflicts. The POTB also operated under the expected confusion that comes with ownership of a new

Touring on Steel Wheels

Excursion train operators can take comfort in a trend back to traveling by rail. These figures reveal the total passenger count—arrivals and departures—on Amtrak trains serving Oregon during the fiscal years shown.

1987	451,543
1988	486,099
1989	464,757
1990	473,522
1991	497,335
1992	496,929

Oregon Coastline Express & Spirit of Oregon *Locomotive Roster*

OCE #701, Alco C415
(ex-Columbia & Cowlitz, built 1968)
OCE #702, Alco C415
(ex-Columbia & Cowlitz, and ex-SP before that—built 1968)
OCE #700 "Lil' Toot Toot," GE 65T Switcher
(ex-U.S. Army, built 1943)
OCE #701B, Morrison-Knudsen slug unit
(ex-Columbia & Cowlitz, rebuilt 1973 from ex-BN Alco S6 #750; now out of service)

Illustration by Deborah A. Winter.

Above—On the magnificent shoreline of Nehalem Bay in September 1989, Oregon Coastline Express #702 runs around its two-car train at Wheeler prior to beginning the 22-mile return trip to Tillamook. Part of the charm of this operation was what the crew told the passengers before uncoupling from the train: "If you don't wave to the train crew, the engineer may decide to head home without you!"

Left—"Lil' Toot Toot," the Oregon Coastline Express caboose tour train, rolls past one of Tillamook's giant blimp hangars. The train, being pulled by a GE 65T diesel, is on a trial run, May 1, 1990. The train was created especially to provide tourists with a unique opportunity to visit the landmark hangars. Two ex-BN cabooses were renovated for the project; each carries 32 passengers.
Collection of Oregon Coastline Express.

railroad—which is basically what the POTB had after buying the SP line to Hillsboro. Although Oregon Coastline Express signed a 10-year lease in February 1990 that authorized excursion train operations on port-owned tracks, the tourist carrier ran into some serious complications. Incidents included the red-flagging of an OCE train, leaving passengers and crew stranded on the line; and holding a tour train for over an hour at a remote station, waiting for a freight to come through. And there were two minor derailments involving excursion trains, leading the POTB to conclude, fairly or unfairly, that the passenger cars were damaging the railroad's physical plant.

Further difficulty stemmed from a decision by the Port of Tillamook Bay to bring in employees from Yakima, Washington, to assist with track repair. Unhappy local workers noted that the railroad was purchased partly with Oregon lottery funds, and the primary purpose of such funds was to provide jobs for Oregonians. Port manager Lon Lasher responded by explaining that the line needed expert repair work, and expert help wasn't available in Tillamook.

As a result of the turmoil, and not wanting to be caught in the middle of a labor dispute, OCE suspended service for one week, May 17-24, 1990—almost immediately after the prime tourist season had begun. During this time, the owners of Oregon Coastline Express seriously considered closing the service completely and pulling out of Tillamook. The city of Hillsboro in particular had been wooing OCE with attractive offers in an attempt to get them to move their business to Hillsboro—"lock, stock, and barrel."

Following the one week "cooling off" period, the POTB's top management assured OCE that they were enthusiastically behind the tourist train concept, and would cooperate to insure smooth, successful, and safe operations. In turn, OCE agreed to alter its schedule to accommodate track repairs being undertaken by the Port of Tillamook Bay. This included temporarily ending all service on Mondays, and limiting trains on other days to one run a day instead of a preferred two a day.

There was optimism that the Steeles' excursion trains could turn a profit and they haven't given up trying: an experimental Oregon Coastline Express dinner train between Batterson and Rockaway

Beach, on September 1, 1990, proved to be a success. And later, OCE ran a special "Wine, Cheese, and Autumn Leaves" train on October 20, 1990, called the *Tillamook Flyer*. It rolled over former SP Tillamook Branch track between Wheeler and Enright, while passengers were treated to wine, cheese, smoked meats, and crackers.

Unfortunately, the news out of Tillamook later was not as promising. During March 1991, Bob Steele announced that OCE would not operate excursion trains for two primary reasons: the liability insurance policy proved much too costly, and the POTB would not allow Oregon Coastline Express to conduct twice-a-day runs over the route, due to heavy track rehabilitation work and an increase in freight train movements. These factors hurt the company's profitability. As a result, the "Rock Coast Route" between Tillamook and Wheeler, which had shown promise in 1989-1990, seemed destined to again stand silent except for the occasional freight train.

There was hope that the Oregon Coastline Express would continue service later in 1991 or 1992, but a new, complicating twist came into play. Another operator, calling its train the "Oregon Coast Explorer," began running along POTB rails between Wheeler and Garibaldi, with the blessing of the Port of Tillamook Bay—despite the fact the Steeles held a lease for exclusive tourist operations. Passengers were carried along the coast in a self-propelled Budd "rail bus" that had been used in commuter service by the New Jersey Transit Authority. Obviously, there wasn't room for two tour train operations along the coast, and something had to give.

After suspension of the Oregon Coastline Express excursion trains in late 1990, Bob and Vickie invested almost two years building the promised luxury dinner train. They were getting ready to come back from their hiatus, and had even put their house in Oceanside up for sale to help finance the plush dinner train. But when the hangar burned, they almost saw their dream go up in smoke—literally.

"I got a phone call at a quarter to 11 one night," Bob recalls. One of the landmark blimp hangars was on fire, and the refurbished dining cars were resting on a siding next to the burning structure. With two years of effort on the line, Steele raced to the scene in his pickup truck and jumped into a locomotive,

Above—Crews rebuild two former BN cabooses for use on the "Mini Express" caboose train in 1989.
Collection of Oregon Coastline Express.

Left—In November 1992, Bob Steele applies Kleer-Kote to one of his C415s being prepared to pull the Spirit of Oregon dinner train. The locomotive is ex-Columbia & Cowlitz #701.

Above right—On September 2, 1990, OCE #700 moves up to couple onto a caboose train for sightseers. In the background, POTB SD9 #4381 waits for the tiny locomotive to clear before bringing its consist of two empty grain hoppers into what's left of the former SP freight yard in Tillamook.

planning to haul the cars away from the flames.

The first obstacle Steele had to overcome was the police. "They were trying to arrest me to keep me out of danger," Bob explains. But Steele went with his instincts. He shouted to the police, "You can arrest me if you can catch me!" Then he started up the locomotive and tried to pull the cars away from the flames.

"I was just about ready to pull out with my cars when some power lines fell onto the tracks in front of the engine," he says. "Sparks were flying all around. Finally they shut the power off and I was able to get the cars out of there before they were burned."

After this trial by fire, the Steeles—with their new *Spirit of Oregon* dinner train—are setting up headquarters in Roy, a farming community on the Tillamook Branch a few miles west of Hillsboro. Weekend dining excursions began with a packed champagne brunch train on St. Valentine's Day, February 14, 1993. The train travels along a 27-mile route between Roy and Cochran.

"We expect to hire 35-45 employees once we're in full operation," says Vickie. Crew members, chefs, servers, and ticket sellers will be hired.

Two Alco C415s—formerly Columbia & Cowlitz Railway #701 and #702—will do the pulling. OCE C415 #702 is the same locomotive that worked the "Rock Coast Route"; both locomotives were built in 1968. In addition, four passenger cars have been restored for the dinner train project, which includes two dining cars, a bar car, and a kitchen car. The cars are luxurious, with mahogany doors and framing, delicate lamps from France, and leather, carpet, and brass furnishings throughout. There is even a dance floor in the bar car.

"Dancing is a good draw; seniors will love it," says Vickie.

The Steeles have completely rewired the passenger cars, and rebuilt the brakes, the electrical generator, and trucks on all four cars.

"We're not messing around with the old," explains Bob. "We don't want a mechanical nightmare. This will be the finest dinner train in the United States."

Featuring a five-course meal, the regularly scheduled dinner excursion rolls every Friday and Saturday evening, with a morning brunch train on Saturdays and Sundays. If the train—which seats a maximum of 136 diners, each paying $65 apiece for dinner or $50 for brunch—operates at capacity, an annual revenue of over $1 million is possible.

Colleen Cornish, operations manager for the Forest Grove Chamber of Commerce, sees benefits in having the dinner train nearby. "It could be an excellent draw, to show people what Washington County and the Forest Grove area have to offer," she says.

"I think the Portland area is ready for this," Bob emphasizes. "If you go out to a nice restaurant in Portland, it's going to be 60 bucks anyway. The *Spirit of Oregon* will be done nicely and elegantly—plus you'll have the experience of the ride."

"Tillamook Celebrities"—Some Bob Steele renovation projects

Midnight Sun Express—Four cars. Originally Southern Pacific bi-level gallery (commuter) cars built by Pullman-Standard in 1969. Tillamook Railcar Repair rebuilt two observation domes (including installing 6-ft. x 7-ft. windows) to seat 90 passengers; also rebuilt were two kitchen cars—one to pair with each observation car. All four cars, known as "Ultra-Domes," went to Alaska after refurbishing in May 1988, and operate between Anchorage and Fairbanks. Car reference numbers: SP #3734 became kitchen car TAIX #7080; SP #3740 became observation car TAIX #7081; SP #3744 became kitchen car TAIX #7082; SP #3745 became observation car TAIX #7083.

Oregon Coastline Express—Two cars. Originally SP bi-level gallery coaches built in 1955. These were made into excursion train cars, each seating 94 passengers. Bob Steele & Associates completed this project in May 1989, and the excursion train began operating immediately thereafter, running between Tillamook and Wheeler on part of the ex-SP Tillamook Branch. The cars were named *Hebo* and *Neah-Kah-Nie*.

Loram Rail Grinding Service—Two cars. Originally Southern Pacific bi-level commuter cars, built in 1955. These were made into double-deck bunkhouse cars, including on-board showers, for rail maintenance crews. Completed and hauled out of Tillamook in July 1989. The coaches are unnamed.

Rail Ventures—Three cars. *Imperial Drive*, built in 1942 for C&NW, was used as a troop sleeper during World War II, and later served on long-haul passenger trains. It was built as a four-bedroom/two-drawing room, business-car/sleeper by Pullman. Rail Ventures renamed it *Yerba Buena*. A heavy dose of luxury was added in the upgrading of the car.

The *City of Cleveland*, built in 1950 for Nickel Plate, was renamed *Montecito* by Rail Ventures. It is a bedroom/diner, complete with wood stove.

Homestead, built in 1950 for Seaboard Air Line, has been renamed *Bella Vista* by Rail Ventures. It is an 11-bedroom sleeper.

Holland America Westours—Two cars. A group of cars, including these two, were built in 1954 as full-length dome cars (85-ft. long) by Budd. First owned by AT&SF, after retirement they were sold to Auto-Train in 1971. Some were subsequently sold to Delaware Otsego Corporation for excursions in the Binghamton, New York, area. Westours Motorcoaches, Inc. (a subsidiary of Holland America Line) bought seven of these dome cars in December 1985. Two were brought to Tillamook to be rebuilt and refurbished as "McKinley Explorers" for use on the Alaska Railroad's Anchorage-Fairbanks trains. Completed in May 1988, the two cars were named *Susitna* and *Kashwitna*. Car reference numbers: *Susitna* was Santa Fe #507, and later Auto-Train #540; *Kashwitna* was Santa Fe #553, later Auto-Train #515, and later still NYSW (Delaware Otsego) #502.

Burlington Northern—One car. Originally a roomette and lounge car, built by Pullman in 1958 for Soo Line, which named it *Minneapolis*. Great Northern purchased the car in 1966, and consequently Burlington Northern inherited it in the 1970 GN-NP-CB&Q-SP&S merger, renaming it *Columbia River*. Bob Steele & Associates repaired and upgraded the car after it was damaged in a sideswiping by a boxcar. Completed and shipped out in September 1989.

Princess Tours—Four cars, which are former Milwaukee Road "Super Domes." These Milwaukee Road observation coaches, built in 1952 by Pullman-Standard, were billed as the largest dome cars ever made, hence the name "Super Domes." Only 10 came off the assembly line, and they were placed in service on Milwaukee Road's *Olympian Hiawatha* trains between Chicago and the West Coast.

Prior to the Bob Steele & Associates overhaul, the cars were acquired by Tour Alaska, and had been in service between Anchorage and Fairbanks on the Alaska Railroad. All four were renovated by Steele for Princess Tours luxury trains (Tour Alaska no longer exists). They carry 60 passengers on the dome level, and another 20 in the dining salon on the lower level. The cars were completed in April 1990.

Milwaukee Road #50 was purchased by Canadian National in 1964 and named *Jasper*, and later was renamed *Mount Foraker* by Tour Alaska, and given serial number TAIX #7092.

Milwaukee Road #52 also was bought by Canadian National in 1964, and named *Columbia*. Tour Alaska renamed it *Mount McKinley*, assigning it serial number TAIX #7090.

Milwaukee Road #56 likewise was purchased by Canadian National in 1964, and called *Fraser*. Tour Alaska renamed it *Mount Susitna*, with serial number TAIX #7091.

Milwaukee Road #59 was acquired by Amtrak in 1971 and given serial number 9383. Tour Alaska renamed it *Mount St. Elias*, and assigned it serial number TAIX #7093.

Sparks fly from a welder's torch as employees work to refurbish dome cars for "Princess Tours" in the summer of 1990.
Collection of Oregon Coastline Express.

The so-called *California Sun Express* service between Los Angeles and Oakland, which initially used these renovated cars, was discontinued at the end of July 1990. Much too quickly, it seems; the concept was never given a legitimate chance. These extremely expensive cars—each cost $900,000 to overhaul—were thereupon sent to Alaska, where business is flourishing.

Transcisco Tours. A fleet of ex-SP, bi-level gallery cars were reborn in Bob Steele's shop as luxury excursion cars for deluxe rail cruises between San Jose, California, and Reno, Nevada, via Tahoe. The elegant 32-seat dome cars of this *Sierra 49er Express* tour train offered gourmet dining, private lounges, and even dancing, with colored lights and live music. These cars sport impressive candy-apple red exteriors, and on the inside feature mahogany paneling, brass appointments, and plush, spacious seating. Service began on December 7, 1990, with a pair of 3,600 h.p. ex-BN F45s providing the power. However, after only five months, Transcisco Tours announced the cancellation of its luxury "Reno Fun Train" tours for financial reasons. The passenger cars are to be leased or sold.

Spirit of Oregon Dinner Train. Bob Steele purchased four cars to get this project under way. A Great Northern 200-series baggage car, built in GN's shops at St. Cloud, Minnesota, in 1950, has been converted into the kitchen car for the *Spirit of Oregon* dinner train. This car is somewhat unusual because one end was originally designed to swing out on two hinges for loading automobiles.

Two former Northern Pacific coaches—NP #505 and NP #507—were built by Pullman-Standard in 1947. Originally constructed as 56-seat coaches with an eight-seat smoking lounge, these cars were commonly used on the *North Coast Limited* trains running between Portland and Seattle. There were a total of 18 of these cars built, numbered 500-517. Two of these cars have been reborn as dining cars for the *Spirit of Oregon*, and Steele is reportedly considering the purchase of ex-NP #508 as well.

The *Spirit of Oregon* bar car has a strange history. It was built by American Car & Foundry in 1945 to serve as a hospital car for the U.S. Army, but World War II ended before it could be put into service. The Alaska Railroad bought three of these hospital cars and had them rebuilt into observation/diner/lounge cars by the Puget Sound Barge & Dredge Company in Seattle. Steele purchased this car—Alaska Railroad #10—and renovated it to serve as the bar car for the *Spirit of Oregon*.

These four cars have all been named for key communities in the area where the dinner train will be operating. The bar car is *Banks*, the kitchen car, *Hillsboro*, and the two dining cars, *Portland* and *Beaverton*.

Top—Rail Ventures passenger cars "Yerba Buena" (nee "Imperial Drive," C&NW) and "Bella Vista" (nee "Homestead," Seaboard Air Line), behind Amtrak's southbound Coast Starlight, pause near the depot in Eugene, Oregon, on October 1, 1989. These two fancy cars—fresh from renovation in Bob Steele's passenger car repair facility in Tillamook—are bound for San Diego and the American Association of Private Railroad Car Owners convention.

Bottom—Interior of BN private car "Columbia River" after renovation.

CHAPTER 5
TRACKS INTO SANTIAM COUNTRY

Burlington Northern's Santiam Branch and
Southern Pacific's Mill City Branch

Every week, a parade of short freight trains rumbles past Southern Pacific's abandoned train-order station in Lebanon, on SP's Mill City Branch. Just east of the battered station, at Sweet Home Junction, the track cuts in two directions. One set of rails—owned by SP—leads to the northeast, while the other set—owned by Burlington Northern—goes southeast. The BN track, known as the Santiam Branch, roughly parallels the South Santiam River all the way to the end of the line at Foster. Southern Pacific's line, meanwhile, continues as far as Mill City along a route that follows the course of the North Santiam River.

Beyond Lebanon, these two rural routes meander through a series of backwater stations with names such as Narrows, Waterloo, and Sweet Home on the BN; and Crabtree, Brewster, Shelburn, and Griggs on the SP. As is typical of Oregon's extensive network of Willamette Valley feeder track, lumber is the predominant commodity being moved over both lines.

Burlington Northern's 31.9-mile Santiam Branch and Southern Pacific's 49.5-mile Mill City Branch are similar in many respects. Both lines are little more than footnotes to their parent roads' widespread operations (BN owns some 25,000 miles of track, while SP, with the D&RGW included, possesses about 15,000 miles). Both branchlines owe their continued existence to the health of the timber industry in Linn County, where virtually all of the trackage is situated. In recent years, both routes have been offered for sale in package deals that included other branches in the

region. And both roads base crews and motive power (normally SD9s in SP's case; GP38-2s or GP9s for BN) for local trains at separate switching yards in Albany. A city with a population of 25,000, Albany is located on SP's Valley Line and BN's Oregon Electric Branch. All trains moving over SP's Mill City Branch and BN's Santiam Branch originate in Albany.

According to the Burlington Northern timetable for this district, the Santiam Branch begins in BN's Albany Yard. BN trains leaving Albany for stations to the east, however, must pass through SP's freight yard, and at Page, one mile south of Albany, trains are switched from the SP mainline. BN then continues on 13 miles of SP trackage to get to Sweet Home Junction in Lebanon.

Burlington Northern's acquisition of trackage rights on the SP right-of-way between Albany and Lebanon reportedly goes back to 1911. In that year, a dispute developed between the Pacific Great Western Railway, backed by the Oregon Electric, and the Willamette Pacific Railroad, controlled by Southern Pacific, over which would build a new line between Eugene and Marshfield (Coos Bay). Both companies coveted a transportation corridor to serve the growing towns and tap the lucrative natural resources available along Oregon's central coast. The controversy wasn't settled until SP offered to let Oregon Electric trains use SP's Albany to Lebanon trackage, and promised not to block the future construction of an anticipated OE branch from Lebanon to Sweet Home. In return, OE backed away from a planned Pacific Coast extension, and SP gained exclusive access to develop what is now the relatively profitable Coos Bay Branch.

BN's Santiam Branch Local—the "BN Logger"—heads west out of Foster, at the end of the Santiam Branch. Drawing the assignment is BN GP9 #1741, a rust-scarred workhorse that is showing its age. The date is March 27, 1991.

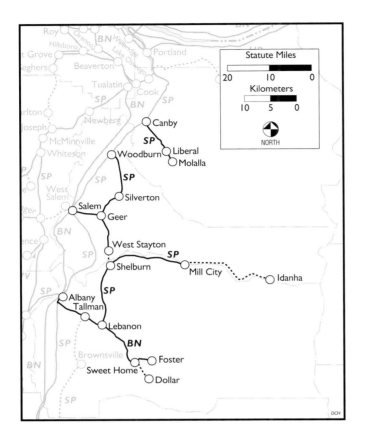

Burlington Northern's Santiam Branch, and Southern Pacific's Mill City Branch,
West Stayton Branch, Geer Branch, and Molalla Branch

Burlington Northern's Santiam Branch, at one time known as the Foster Branch, was opened to Sweet Home and Foster in 1932 by the Oregon Electric. (A short southeastward extension was also constructed—from Sweet Home to Dollar—but this mileage saw its last train in 1961.) All the trackage was originally built to reach new stands of timber, and lumber remains its lifeblood today. The Santiam Branch roadbed remains in good shape for a feeder line. Rail is primarily 90-lb., with crushed rock as ballast over most of the route, and thousands of new ties were installed in 1986.

The Oregon Public Utility Commission classifies the route as "Secure Minus" (meaning traffic over the line appears stable for at least the next five years), but makes note of some threats to the traffic base. Besides the potential loss of traffic to reloading facilities, a marketing shift away from direct rail use (that is,

boxcars and flatcars) to intermodal service (trailers or containers) by any of the active mills on this line could severely reduce the number of carloads moving over the line. In the early 1990s, train activity remains steady with a number of shippers, including Willamette Industries and Smurfit's particleboard plant at Sweet Home. A Champion Lumber Company facility in Lebanon has closed, although the site retains its trackage and is being developed by the city of Lebanon as an industrial park, keeping alive the possibility of new shippers locating there.

The main Santiam Branch customer is Willamette Industries, which has mills alongside BN rails in Foster, Waterloo, and Bauman. There is also a large Georgia-Pacific facility at Weldwood, on the outskirts of Lebanon; and a Boise Cascade plywood mill near Sweet Home.

On the downside, a Willamette Industries sawmill

Santiam Branch (BN)
Stations

Albany .... MP 96.5
Lebanon (OE Siding) .... MP 14.8
Weldwood .... MP 15.9
Bauman .... MP 20.8
Boise Cascade Plywood .... MP 26.0
Sweet Home .... MP 29.0
Foster .... MP 31.9

in Sweet Home that employed 80 workers closed in early 1989, followed by the April 1990 closure of Midway Veneer, likewise owned by Willamette Industries. Another of BN's Sweet Home shippers, Pleasant Valley Plywood, recently shut down as well. All three closures were due to high raw material costs and a declining availability of logs. This erosion of business has not severely impaired the health of BN's Santiam Branch for now, yet the losses are a serious and troubling sign of the times.

Burlington Northern, as is the case with Southern Pacific, normally employs just one locomotive to work the line; there is rarely a need for extra power over the relatively lean route. The Santiam Branch Local, called the "BN Logger," leaves Albany every weekday morning for Foster, carrying empty boxcars and flatcars east for the remaining shippers along the way. Loaded cars, anywhere from 8 to 15 on an average haul, are gathered up and brought back west. From Albany, customers' lumber loads are carried north to Portland and Vancouver, Washington—via the Oregon Electric Branch—for shipment to all points; some cars are handed off to SP at either Lebanon or Albany.

Turning now to the other branchline described in this chapter, Southern Pacific's Mill City Branch features a handful of rail users near the end of track between Lyons (MP 719.3) and Mill City (MP 725.7), including Frank Lumber, which is the most active shipper in the area. On Tuesdays and Thursdays, SP sends a train called the "Albany Roustabout" to handle customers on the branch—Freres Lumber and Young & Morgan Lumber in Lyons, along with Frank Lumber and North Santiam Plywood in Mill City. In the words of Dick Kester, an SP man for 36 years and

a conductor based in Albany, the Albany Roustabout earned its name "because we'd go everywhere." In fact, after switching customers in Lebanon, it's not unusual for the Albany Roustabout to run all the way to Mill City—another 37 miles—just to serve the Frank Lumber mill near the end of the route.

"Sometimes it seemed like the Mill City Branch was just a long spur into Frank Lumber," recalls Scott Pirie, an SP engineer who worked the line until 1992.

Alternating with running on the Mill City Branch on Tuesdays and Thursdays, the Albany Roustabout keeps busy working south on the Valley Line as far as Junction City on Mondays, Wednesdays, and Fridays. The train has a four-member crew, and requires a caboose due to a two-mile backing move to reach a James River Corporation paper plant in Halsey.

Crews go on duty at 7:30 a.m., and, on the days they venture to Mill City, run close to going over the 12-hour work limit before returning to Albany. With switching at Lebanon and the time it takes to get to distant mills in Lyons and Mill City, the train sometimes doesn't get back to Albany until 6 or 7 p.m. The Willamette Industries plant in Lebanon was perhaps the Mill City branchline's best customer, as it provided about eight boxcars of lumber a week. In July 1991, however, the mill closed its doors, and this could have a significant impact on the long-range health of the line.

Reliable shippers in Lebanon include Entek, Inc., a business that manufactures parts for batteries; and, right across the tracks, Pennington Seed. Pennington is a new shipper that put in a long siding to its loading dock in 1989 and is shipping boxcars of seed. Both firms are adjacent to the small SP yard in Lebanon. Further west, at Irvinville (near Tallman), there is a seasonal shipper of grass seed.

The bad news is the same as that facing BN's Santiam Branch. SP has been losing customers in recent years—not so much to trucks, but to mill closures. In 1984, Mount Jefferson Plywood in Lyons closed down, followed in 1985 by a Willamette Industries plywood mill at Griggs, about six miles northeast of Lebanon.

The Griggs loss was especially damaging. Not only did it eliminate 131 millworker positions, it forced SP to sharply curtail operations over the line. Until the facility shut down, the well-named "Snow Peak

Above—BN GP38-2 #2083 backs toward a loading shed to spot boxcars at the Willamette Industries sawmill in Foster at the end of the Santiam Branch, May 1989. GP38-2s are the primary power seen on BN's Oregon branchlines, and this afternoon is no exception. Trains based in Albany make the 32-mile journey to Foster five days a week.

Right—On July 19, 1990, the BN Logger arrives at Lebanon Junction with five loaded cars. BN GP9 #1875, although more than three decades old, has ably handled the day's switching assignments. At Lebanon Junction, BN's Santiam Branch Local must pause to get clearance from SP before advancing onto SP's Mill City Branch. BN trains use trackage rights from SP to get from Albany to Lebanon where the two lines diverge.

Logger" trains came to Griggs daily; they carried logs from there to a mill in Dallas. At that time, Griggs was the most productive station on the branch beyond Lebanon. Indeed, SP had based a locomotive and caboose at Lebanon to expedite local switching, until the loss of Griggs as an active customer. (Similarly, until 1986, BN maintained a locomotive at Sweet Home to facilitate service to the many mills in that area.) Consequently, since 1985, service has been cut back to twice a week.

A number of mills on both SP's Mill City Branch and BN's Santiam Branch have closed temporarily to retool and refit in order to handle smaller logs, a wise move when considering that large logs are getting scarcer all the time. Mills in Lebanon, Sweet Home, and Foster have announced this action.

The status of the Mill City Branch has been broken down to two parts, according to the PUC. The segment between Albany and Lebanon is regarded as "Secure," meaning the line appears healthy for more than five years. Not surprisingly, given the potential

for further mill closures, the trackage from Lebanon to Mill City is listed as "Questionable." Physically, much of the Mill City Branch is in good condition. Between Page and Lebanon (11.5 miles), the physical plant would put some mainlines to shame. Most of the ties are almost new, and the track itself is 112-lb. continuous welded rail, with a bed of crushed rock.

The remainder of the branchline, Lebanon to Mill City (37.2 miles), is in poorer condition. The rail is primarily 75-lb. and 80-lb., and many of the ties, notably in the Lyons area, are over 50 years old and splintering badly. The ballast on the roadbed beyond Lebanon is a combination of crushed rock and pit run materials.

The speed limit on the branch is 40 mph maximum, with slower restrictions in a number of places; east of Lebanon, speed limits range between 10 mph and 30 mph. In the late 1980s, SP officials stated that they would probably place the segment between Lebanon and Mill City into Category 1 (subject to abandonment within three years), but did

Mill City Branch (SP)
Stations

not do so. Instead, in December 1991, the carrier announced it was interested in selling or leasing several of its Oregon branchlines—including the line to Mill City.

SP has helped its own cause somewhat by offering new, more competitive rates for Oregon customers. SP reduced its per-car lumber rates by 10 percent for loads originating in Oregon and destined for points on SP lines in Arizona, California, New Mexico, and Nevada. Some firms on the Mill City route were hauling their goods to a BN reload center in Salem to take advantage of BN single-line tariffs, so SP wisely adjusted its rates downward to stem this siphoning of tonnage onto BN.

Recently there has been a new challenge for SP's marketing department. On July 6, 1990, three of Southern Pacific's chief competitors—Santa Fe, Union Pacific, and Burlington Northern—signed the "Northwest Passage" agreement. This contract allows any one of these railroads to move shipments using the other two carriers' trains and tracks through a five-state region—Oregon, California, Washington, Arizona, and New Mexico. Apparently, the primary purpose of this deal is to provide shippers in the Northwest and Southwest with an attractive alternative to transporting goods by interstate trucking or the Southern Pacific. It remains to be seen how SP

will counter this development.

SP's track between Lebanon and Albany was built in 1880 as the appropriately named Albany & Lebanon Railroad, under the auspices of the Oregon & California Railroad. SP acquired the Albany & Lebanon in 1890.

In 1878, the line to Mill City was originally envisioned by the founder of the Oregon Pacific Railroad, Colonel Thomas E. Hogg, as an extension from Yaquina Bay (on the Pacific Ocean near Newport and Toledo) over the Cascade Range. Hogg's lofty hope was to connect with transcontinental carriers in Boise, Idaho, in an attempt to make the Oregon Pacific a major player in West Coast transportation. A total of 138 miles of the Oregon Pacific Railroad's "Webfoot Route" was completed eastward from the coast by 1889, and reached Idanha, a mere 12 miles from the summit of the Cascade Range. But the dream stalled in 1890 due to financial failure, and the rails never advanced beyond Idanha.

Had the ambitious project been completed, it could have significantly changed Oregon's history. Instead, the track now comes to an unglamorous dead end in Mill City, in clear view of snow-capped peaks. The trackage finally ended up in SP's hands when it purchased the property in 1907, thereby taking deed to what is today the Mill City Branch. The western-most segment, between Albany and Toledo via Corvallis, is now SP's Toledo Branch (see chapter six).

In 1953, a section of the right-of-way extension beyond Mill City was flooded by the Army Corps of Engineers' Detroit Dam project, leaving parts of the old roadbed—and Colonel Hogg's dreams—under 100 feet of water. As a result of the flooding, the line was pared back first to Gates, two miles east of Mill City, and later to Mill City, where it tenuously remains today.

Due to abandonments on adjacent feeder lines, the Mill City Branch has undergone significant alterations in recent years. Prior to 1973, service on the branch originated in Springfield, located 80.4 miles to the south. Trains moved north-south on the line between Springfield and Woodburn, via Lebanon Junction (now known as Tallman). Trains cut onto the present day version of the Mill City Branch at Shelburn and then moved east from there to the end of the line.

Above—Southern Pacific's Mill City Local arrives in SP's small freight yard in Lebanon, September 27, 1990, behind SD9 #4364. The crew is returning to Albany after working several lumber mills between Lebanon and Mill City, 38 miles down the line. Following the SP freight into the yard is BN's counterpart train, the BN Logger, also on its way back to Albany. Both trains will pause to do a bit of work in the yard, including picking up carloads of grass seed from Pennington Seed Company, a firm that enjoys direct service from two railroads, a rarity in Oregon.

Right—The SP Albany Roustabout at Lebanon, switching the Willamette Industries mill in June 1991.

Mill City Branch (SP)
Direct Traffic Control Block

Fry Block .... West MP 691.5; East MP 687.3

Softwood Lumber Shipments from Oregon by Rail
(in board feet)

1988	2.6 billion
1989	2.4 billion
1990	1.9 billion
1991	1.6 billion
1992	1.5 billion

But the route essentially ceased to exist when, in 1973, a flood weakened a bridge over the McKenzie River at Armitage (between Coburg and Springfield) and the southern part of the line was taken out of service shortly thereafter.

The 30 miles of track south from Tallman to a lumber mill at Wilkins was renamed the Wilkins Branch—all of which was abandoned in 1985. After the 1973 flood and until its abandonment, the Wilkins Branch too was served by crews based in Albany.

Also in the early 1970s, a 3.4-mile stretch of track from Shelburn to West Stayton was abandoned, cutting off the northern part of the line. Out of necessity, routing to Mill City had to be reconfigured; instead of originating from Springfield or Woodburn, Albany Yard was assigned the duty of servicing Lebanon and Mill City.

Eventually, to reflect operating reality, the entire 8.8-mile Tallman Branch (Albany-Tallman) was combined with the Tallman-Mill City segment. Thus, the "new" Mill City Branch extends from Mill City through Lebanon and Tallman to Albany, and totals 49.5 miles.

The remaining pieces of the old Woodburn-Springfield line were given names of their own. Woodburn to West Stayton became the 31.7-mile West Stayton Branch, which is still in use serving a variety of shippers in Mount Angel, Silverton, Stayton, and Woodburn. Woodburn used to be the

At one time or another, Southern Pacific's Valley Line carries virtually all of the tonnage generated by SP's Oregon branchline network. On March 26, 1991, a northbound freight roars through Page, with GP40-2 #7966 on the point. Page is where SP's Mill City Branch connects with the Valley Line.

home base for operations on this branchline, but now the West Stayton local originates out of Salem. The West Stayton Turn—by way of either the 6.5-mile Geer Branch (Salem-Geer) or the Valley Line from Salem to Woodburn and south from there—visits these towns three days a week, hauling out corn syrup, lumber, canned goods, and frozen foods.

Another line in the immediate vicinity of the West Stayton Branch, although not physically connected, is SP's 10.4-mile Molalla Branch. This line begins on the Valley Line in Canby—about half-way between Woodburn and Oregon City—and extends southeast to Molalla, a small timber town in Clackamas County. Like so many other Oregon lines, the Molalla Branch depends almost completely on lumber mills to sustain operations, but agricultural goods also move over the route; Satrum-Dybvad Milling keeps a steady flow of grain hoppers moving to its facility in Liberal, three miles up the line from Molalla. The primary wood products shipper is RSG Forest Products, also in Liberal. Southern Pacific crews out of Brooklyn Yard in Portland service this branch several times a week. The entire line, built with 75-lb. rail, is classified as FRA Excepted track. Accordingly, all train movements over the Molalla Branch are restricted to 10 mph.

The Mill City Branch and the Santiam Branch—two historic routes in Oregon's "Santiam Country"—

Above—The BN Logger, led by GP38 #2076, nears Weldwood on the Santiam Branch.

Above right—SP SD9 #4389 leads the Mill City Local onto a trestle near the end of the branchline in Mill City, Oregon, May 25, 1989. After switching out Frank Lumber Company, the train will begin the return trip to Albany.

Right—On March 26, 1991, Amtrak's southbound Coast Starlight rushes past the BN Logger, which is waiting on a siding at Albany on SP's Valley Line after working the nearby Santiam Branch.

face an uncertain future; a future inextricably tied to the viability of the wood products industry in the Northwest. The timber industry is in transition and the rail lines are facing some of the consequences. The Western Wood Products Association, based in Portland, reported a 6.3 percent decline in softwood lumber shipments by rail from Oregon in 1992, as compared to 1991 figures.

As long as the timber supply and the nation's overall economy remains reasonably stable, trains in the Santiam area will, no doubt, continue running. But if there are too few logs to go around, or if the market slumps sharply, these two scenic branches—like many Northwest lumber mills—might shut down permanently.

CHAPTER 6
116-MILE LOCAL

Southern Pacific's Toledo Branch

Six heavy road units, with a GP40-2 in the lead, race north out of Eugene Yard pulling a long freight. The train bulls across the floor of Oregon's Willamette Valley on Southern Pacific's fast, CTC-regulated mainline, apparently headed for Portland. Forty-one miles later, however, the train slows as it enters the SP freight yard at Albany. Instead of continuing northward, the train cuts west onto a well-built branchline about half a mile north of Albany's Amtrak depot.

From this junction in Albany, the Toledo Branch begins, and the Toledo Local—more commonly known by the name "Toledo Hauler"—operates compass west (considered east by SP timetable) to Georgia-Pacific's vast, 100-acre paper mill 75 miles away in Toledo. With a population of 3,500, Toledo is a quintessential Northwest mill town.

The Toledo Branch is not just another lumber line in the outback of Oregon. It is, according to an Oregon Public Utility Commission report, the "best of Southern Pacific's Oregon branchlines." That's high praise, and the line's specifications warrant it. The entire branch is laid with 132-lb. rail, a fair portion of it continuous welded rail (CWR). The track is well-ballasted with crushed rock, and the ties, for the most part, are in excellent shape. Direct traffic control blocks govern train movements. Officially, this 75.8-mile branchline begins in Albany Yard at MP 690.9, and terminates in Toledo, at MP 766.7. But in practice, the SP's Toledo Hauler begins operations in Eugene at MP 647.3, where road power and crews are based.

The Toledo Hauler westbound at Wren, Oregon, December 11, 1989.

The route almost exclusively serves the Georgia-Pacific facility in Toledo, which, indeed, requires a great deal of servicing: each day the plant's 550 employees produce approximately 1,950 tons of linerboard, corrugating medium, and kraft paper. The Toledo Hauler moves out these materials.

Every day except Sunday, Southern Pacific brings into Toledo as many as 20 or 30 carloads of woodchips from Eugene for GP's rotary chip dumper, along with another two dozen or so empty boxcars and a few flatcars slated for the Wheeler Manufacturing Company, another customer based in Toledo. The Wheeler plant ships several carloads of lumber per week, and the huge volume of paper products coming from the GP mill are hauled primarily to California markets; as many as 20,000 cars move over the line in a given year.

Two separate road crews make three round trips per week with the Toledo Hauler. One team works Mondays, Wednesdays, and Fridays; the other reports on Tuesdays, Thursdays, and Saturdays. Going on duty at 5 a.m., crews run non-stop to Albany Yard, where cars are set out for local service. After this task is completed, the train continues to Toledo, usually arriving at about 2 p.m. In Toledo, the crew rests for about eight hours. A switching crew, with an SD9 at their disposal, is stationed there to work the GP mill and make up the return train while the road crew relaxes.

When the Toledo Hauler crew returns to duty, they work through the night to bring the Georgia-Pacific and Wheeler loads and the empty woodchip cars back to Eugene by the next morning. Along the way, outbound cars from shippers served by three different SP locals—the Dawson Local, Dallas Local,

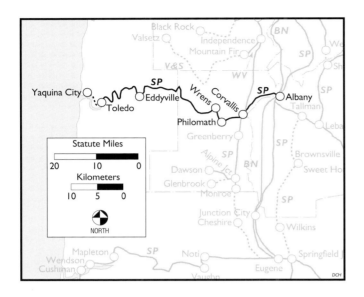

Southern Pacific's Toledo Branch

and Wrens Turn—are collected at Corvallis Junction and carried through to Eugene. In exchange, about every other week a cut of empty woodchip cars slated for the Hull-Oakes mill in Dawson will be left at the junction for the Corvallis-based Dawson Local.

The Eugene-bound Hauler almost always makes it back to Eugene before the Toledo-bound Hauler heads out. This becomes significant given the fact that, on rare occasions, the Toledo Haulers must share their power.

By rail, it is 116 miles between Eugene and Toledo. Forty-one of those miles are expedited mainline running on SP's classy (and relatively flat) Valley Line. Fast freights blast through a series of small farm towns between Eugene and Albany, including Junction City, Harrisburg, and Halsey. But the remaining 75 miles beyond Albany are primarily winding and rugged, and include a difficult climb over the Coast Range.

The mountainous profile of western Oregon explains why SP uses an impressive fleet of diverse—and sometimes offbeat—locomotives on the Toledo Branch. Typical configurations of power for the Toledo Hauler include multiple GP40-2s, SD9s, and TEBU slugs. Certainly not what one would expect to

discover on a "backwoods" branchline!

Leaving Albany, the Toledo Hauler's route immediately carries it over Burlington Northern's Oregon Electric Branch (the SP crosses the BN at the end of a long wooden trestle and unused river swingspan that leads over the Willamette River). Eleven miles later, directly north of Corvallis, the Toledo Branch connects with the West Side Branch at Corvallis Junction. In fact, for 1.2 miles—from south of Corvallis Junction to immediately north of the Corvallis classification yard—the West Side Branch and Toledo Branch overlap.

From Corvallis Junction, trains go right down the middle of Sixth Street in Corvallis, passing automobile traffic on *both* sides of the right-of-way through town before continuing across the Oregon State University campus. (It's a bit surprising there has been no push to create a wide "whistle-free zone" in Corvallis, especially since similar petitions were successful in nearby Eugene and Salem—much to the displeasure of those of us who *appreciate* hearing the sound of trains moving through the night. In any event, the state Public Utility Commission, citing safety considerations, rescinded the whistle bans in 1993.)

Next comes the Coast Range. First, trains proceed

Looming out of a heavy fog, six units of the Toledo Hauler lead a long train toward Toledo on December 12, 1989. This trestle, just west of Albany, crosses the Willamette River—train crews call it the "water ditch"— and a golf course.

through the foothills around Philomath, before eventually reaching Summit, 37 miles east of Toledo and almost exactly at the mid-point on the Toledo Branch. At Summit, trains crest the mountains only to encounter one of the steepest sections of track in Oregon. On the west slope of Summit's 704-ft. pass, the grade is a cruel 2.58 percent; here the TEBUs earn their keep. Five miles further, at Nashville, the profile smooths out considerably while the route crosses and recrosses the Yaquina River several times on the final stretch into Toledo. The roadbed follows the Yaquina River valley for almost 32 miles.

Two alternating power sets are readied in Eugene Yard for use on the Toledo Haulers, and, barring a unit needing repair, the day-to-day lineups tend to vary only slightly. As with the crews, each set of engines makes a round trip shuttle between Eugene and Toledo three times a week. Normally, all the power remains on the point for the entire run, although occasionally extra units are spliced in somewhere in the middle of the train. Now and then, a solid bank of seven or eight SD9s will lead, but usually at least one booster is present, mated to a pair of SP or SSW GP40-2s. The TEBUs, rebuilt from U25Bs, have become a mainstay on both the Toledo Branch and the Coos Bay Branch a few dozen miles to the south. SP has 14 GE-built TEBU road slugs on its roster, and most of them serve in branchline duty in Oregon.

In the early 1970s, SP experimented with SD45s on the Toledo Branch, but these heavier locomotives

The Toledo Hauler, coming down the middle of Sixth Street in Corvallis, August 23, 1990. Six locomotives—five SD9s and a GP9—pull the train on its 116-mile run from Eugene to Toledo. SD9 #4323, with a dented snout, is on the point. Normally GP40-2s are present on this train, with a TEBU slug or two as well.

Toledo Branch (SP)
Stations

proved to be too rough on the track and were soon assigned elsewhere. Adding to the line's history of interesting power mixes is the fact that it was on the Toledo Branch where SP's F-units made their last stand in Oregon. And, even in the 1990s, it's not uncommon to see GP9s working the line.

The Toledo Branch also attracts an unlikely collection of cabooses at times. Along with the standard Southern Pacific and Cotton Belt bay-window models, D&RGW cupola-types have been frequent visitors on the line. In a single week in December 1989, for example, three different Rio Grande waycars were observed: D&RGW #01457, D&RGW #01432, and D&RGW #01420. Burlington Northern cabooses also have seen service on SP's Toledo trackage. But most surprising, even the Soo Line has put in an appearance: Soo caboose #137 was

Above—SP SD9 #4330 services the Georgia-Pacific paper mill and SP yard at Toledo in November 1989.

Below—Crew members exchange greetings as the Toledo Hauler rolls through Corvallis, June 1991. On the left is the Dallas Local waiting for the run up to Corvallis Junction.

Toledo Hauler Power Sets
Week of December 11-16, 1989—
(Monday-Wednesday-Friday)

SSW #7965—GP40-2
SP #1602—TEBU slug
SP #7950—GP40-2
SSW #7964—GP40-2
SP #4407—SD9
SP #4423—SD9

(Tuesday-Thursday-Saturday)

SP #7943—GP40-2
SSW #7966—GP40-2
SP #1601—TEBU slug
SP #7954—GP40-2
SP #1613—TEBU slug
SSW #7967—GP40-2

Week of October 1-6, 1990—
(Monday-Wednesday-Friday)

SP #7952—GP40-2
SP #1601—TEBU slug
SSW #7964—GP40-2
SSW #7967—GP40-2
SP #1602—TEBU slug
SP #7950—GP40-2

(Tuesday-Thursday-Saturday)

SSW #7966—GP40-2
SP #1605—TEBU slug
SSW #7965—GP40-2
SP #4363—SD9
SP #4422—SD9

on the tail of the Toledo Hauler on January 6, 1990—and Soo #144 handled the assignment on January 10, 1990.

As important as the Toledo Haulers are, the branch also hosts some vital activity by a lower profile work train called the Philomath Local, or Wrens Turn. The crew of the Wrens Turn, working with one of the reliable, and ubiquitous, EMD products known as SD9s, goes on duty in Albany at 3:30 p.m., five days a week. They are scheduled to hustle cars as far as a lumber mill at Wrens, 25 miles west of Albany, then return. (Most Oregon maps show this town as Wren—however, SP's timetable refers to it as Wrens.)

There are a number of on-line forest products companies between Philomath and Wrens, and this milk-run local makes all the stops: Midway Forest Products, Diamond-B Lumber, Philomath Forest Products, Leading Plywood, Pacific Softwoods, Smurfit Newsprint, Marys River Lumber. Additionally, the Wrens Turn brings cars from Albany to Corvallis Junction, shoving them onto the wye there for local trains out of Corvallis to collect as needed. The Wrens Turn's schedule also calls for a stop at the small Corvallis classification yard to pick up any carloads brought from customers situated south of Corvallis and served Tuesday and Thursday by the Dawson Local. These cars are then hauled north to Corvallis Junction, and usually left for the nightly Eugene-bound Toledo Hauler. As a result of all this, the Wrens Turn sometimes pulls enough tonnage to rate two SD9s. But more often than not, one locomotive is sufficient.

The origins of SP's Toledo Branch can be traced all the way back to 1878. Colonel Thomas E. Hogg, the New York-based entrepreneur mentioned in chapter five, envisioned a transcontinental line with Corvallis as the key terminal. Beginning at Yaquina Bay, which offered a fairly good natural port, Hogg planned to extend the line east via Corvallis, Albany, and Prineville—crossing first the Coast Range and then the Cascades—and on across the scrub and sagebrush of eastern Oregon to link up with the Union Pacific or another major carrier in Boise, Idaho. This grand, freewheeling project also called for two important branchlines to be constructed: one to Umatilla, Oregon, on the Columbia River, and another to Winnemucca, Nevada, connecting with the Central Pacific.

In 1879, Hogg's laborers started by laying 10 miles of narrow-gauge track west from Corvallis as the first segment of the Corvallis & Yaquina Bay Railroad. But soon after that was finished, Colonel Hogg decided to change to standard-gauge. Construction began anew in 1881. In the interim, the company had changed its identity and became known as the Oregon Pacific Railroad.

In 1885, the first train from Corvallis to Yaquina City came over the line, powered by a Grant 2-4-0 locomotive named Corvallis. No doubt this flattering tribute was in part designed to further fan enthusiasm and garner support in a town hungry for a railroad. Tellingly, Hogg's motto for the Oregon Pacific was "To promise not, but to work," perhaps to silence critics who wanted to know precisely when a segment of the line would finally be opened.

The Yaquina City to Corvallis trackage was the essential beginning to Hogg's dream of linking ocean steamers with a transcontinental railroad to move goods out of the Willamette Valley. On paper at least, Hogg's plan looked sound. The Oregon Pacific's route would slash mileage from long east-west hauls, thereby lowering transportation costs for Oregon wheat. And with the natural harbor at Yaquina Bay, there was a potential opening to overseas trading. It was anticipated that Yaquina City would rival San Francisco as the West Coast's premier transportation hub. To handle the expected business, the Oregon Pacific built a turntable and six-stall locomotive roundhouse at Yaquina City. Steamships tied up at Yaquina Bay's docks, and freight trains worked across the tidelands toward Toledo on a low, open-deck wooden trestle.

The Oregon Pacific's detractors, however, scoffed at Hogg's line with devastatingly derisive comments: "From a rock pile in the Cascades to a mud puddle by the Pacific," one newspaper editor sneered. In his fine book *Railroads down the Valleys*, author Randall Mills responded poignantly to this particular criticism of the Oregon Pacific Railroad:

"But the rock pile marked the sunrise," he wrote in 1950, "and the mud puddle looked toward the Orient. It was such stuff as dreams are made on—it

Corvallis & Eastern #2 rests at Nashville on what later became the SP's Toledo Branch. Workers are loading cordwood fuel onto the locomotive. The #2 was built in 1882, and scrapped by Southern Pacific in 1915.
Collection of Oregon Historical Society, #4.75052.

was the frontier where the ends transcended the means."

The Oregon Pacific's inception was promising, but 12 years after construction began in earnest, and after expenditures of $15 million, a mere 142 miles of the so-called "Webfoot Route" had been completed: it extended from Yaquina City to Idanha, still 12 miles from the summit of the Cascade Range, and hundreds of miles from Boise. The bondholders' patience evaporated. In 1893, Hogg was removed from receivership of the Oregon Pacific.

Yet despite his business failings, Hogg at least seemed sincere in his goals. He made the extreme effort of having a boxcar, with a short section of track, hauled up the Santiam Canyon to Hogg Pass in the Cascades to "hold the franchise" for the Oregon Pacific. A team of horses actually pulled the boxcar back and forth on a few hundred yards of isolated track to keep the never-used claim legal. The boxcar and track sat abandoned in the mountains for decades until, regrettably, a junk dealer finally "salvaged" and scrapped this bizarre piece of history.

In 1897, the property was again reorganized—this time as the Corvallis & Eastern Railway—but still it went nowhere. When forced to sell assets to survive, all thought of laying more track died. In 1907, out of options, the line was sold to the Southern Pacific Railroad.

Had the Corvallis & Eastern been able to endure a few years longer, perhaps with the coming of World War I in Europe there might have been one last shot at completing the line eastward over the Cascades, and thereby altering Oregon's transportation history. But by then SP held title to the trackage.

The war brought blooming prosperity to what SP had named the Yaquina Branch. The U.S. Army desperately needed spruce, an extremely strong wood, for airplane frames. Oregon's central coast was filled with dense stands of spruce trees, and freight trains came to haul timber for the war effort. Ironically, the railroads were helping the fledgling aircraft industry—a future competitor—get a jump start.

As many as 18 trains a day came to Toledo, while logging railroads penetrated into the thick forests here and there near the coast. Light locomotives of the consolidation class were constantly at work, pulling long cuts of log-laden flatcars to an Army-

Toledo Branch (SP)
Direct Traffic Control Blocks

Granger Block	West MP 691.6; East MP 697.0
Ashahr Block	West MP 697.0; East MP 701.1
Flynn Block	West MP 703.6; East MP 712.0
Wrens Block	West MP 712.0; East MP 728.4
Summit Block	West MP 728.4; East MP 745.2
Eddyville Block	West MP 745.2; East MP 762.0

operated mill at Toledo. This project was considered so essential that a thousand troops from "the Spruce Division" were based near Toledo to work in the mill and forests. (Spruce Division soldiers also were stationed on the Olympic Peninsula in Washington, where they likewise logged the forests and operated sawmills.) The Georgia-Pacific plant operating in Toledo today is a direct descendant of the Army's World War I-era facility.

Eventually Southern Pacific split the would-be transcontinental road into two feeder lines, with a branch on each side of the Valley Line; and so it remains into the 1990s. West of Albany, former Oregon Pacific trackage is known as the Toledo Branch; southeast from Albany, via Page, it's the Mill City Branch. Both lines have been trimmed back from their furthest extensions, and the Oregon Pacific's original, direct right-of-way northeast from Albany to Shelburn was abandoned decades ago.

SP pulled out of Yaquina City in 1937, and soon thereafter the branchline's name was changed to reflect its new terminus in Toledo. Yaquina City is now a ghost town. In places, eerie remnants of brine-encrusted wooden trestles still stand in the tidal marshes between Toledo and Newport.

The future of the Toledo Branch, unlike that of so many of the other secondary and feeder lines in Oregon, is simple: as long as the Georgia-Pacific mill remains in operation, the line will almost certainly continue to see steady use. But if the mill goes, the Toledo Haulers will disappear. Not far behind them will be the rails and ties themselves, and the Toledo Branch, like the Yaquina Branch and the "Webfoot Route" preceding it, will pass into memory.

Gone as well—like the forlorn boxcar at the crest of the Cascade mountains—will be the last vestiges of Colonel Hogg's transcontinental ambitions. ▼━

Above—At Ashahr, Oregon, on March 29, 1991, SP's Toledo Hauler heads toward Toledo with a long line of cars powered by five road units: SD9 #4430, GP40-2 #7638, GP40-2 #7965, TEBU slug #1605, and GP40-2 #7949.

Left—Caught at Corvallis, Denver & Rio Grande Western caboose #01457 completes the Toledo Hauler consist, December 12, 1989.

Above left—Power mix on the Toledo Local at Eddyville, December 11, 1989.

Left—SD9 #4419 cuts through the thickly forested Oregon Coast Range landscape as it heads west, Toledo bound, on December 14, 1986.
Photo: Ed Austin, collection of Tom Dill.

Above—The Toledo Hauler glides along Sixth Street in Corvallis, October 1990. SD9 #4363 leads two GP40-2s and a TEBU slug toward the huge Georgia-Pacific paper mill near Toledo.

CHAPTER 7
NORTH WILLAMETTE SHORTLINES

Willamette Valley Railroad and the Willamina & Grand Ronde Railway,
with Southern Pacific connecting lines Willamina Branch, West Side Branch,
Dallas Branch, West Side-Seghers Branch, and Newberg Branch

"Once you get railroading in your blood, it's hard to get it out," says Mike Root. And he should know, because along with his brother David and business partner George Lavacot, he owns two shortline railroads. In fact, it's no overstatement to say that railroading is in the bloodlines of the Root family: their father worked for Union Pacific, their grandfather for the Santa Fe, and Mike and David both worked for a time with Union Pacific in California.

Although generally happy during their time of employment with the Union Pacific, David and Mike eventually decided they wanted to run their *own* railroad and started looking for a suitable shortline to purchase. They wound up with two: the Willamette Valley Railroad and the Willamina & Grand Ronde Railway.

Both of these railroads first came into existence decades ago under the ownership of two different forest products companies. What is today the Willamette Valley Railroad rose from the ashes of a long-time Boise Cascade Corporation operation, while the route of what is now the Willamina & Grand Ronde Railway was for many years owned by International Paper Company. In the early 1990s, both lines continue to owe their existence to the timber industry. Each has depended upon a single lumber mill for virtually all of its respective business, and lumber is normally the only commodity hauled by either carrier.

The Roots began their hunt for a railroad in earnest in the 1970s, after a possible deal for the Quincy Railroad in California fell through. They knew they

wanted to stay in the West, but other than that, their options were open. Ironically, it was while vacationing in Oregon that they decided to go after the eight-mile line between Grand Ronde and Willamina.

The route had been built in the early 1920s, and, before the Root brothers purchased it, was most recently owned by International Paper's Longview, Portland & Northern Railway. The LP&N's track extended from Willamina to Grand Ronde, although years earlier there had also been logging railroads extending west from Grand Ronde. The LP&N was one of several contemporary Oregon shortlines operated or originated by lumber companies—not an unusual phenomenon in timber-rich Oregon. Among others, the list includes the Klamath Northern, owned by Gilchrist Lumber Company; the Oregon, California & Eastern, owned by Weyerhaeuser and now out of service; the Oregon, Pacific & Eastern, owned by Bohemia, Inc., and facing an uncertain future; and the Mount Hood Railroad, built for the Oregon Lumber Company in 1906.

It took a year and a half to close the deal, but in 1980 the last papers were signed and the LP&N became the Willamina & Grand Ronde Railway (WGR). Unfortunately, that same year, an Oregon Public Utility Commission track inspector determined that the entire route needed substantial rehabilitation. In fact, the WGR's roadbed was in deplorable condition. The steel rail was extremely old and frail: 56-lb. to 60-lb., rolled at the turn of the century. To compound the situation, the ties were in poor shape, and drainage and surfacing were bad. It was a mess, and repairs would be costly; the state PUC estimated rehabilitation costs at $167,000 per mile. Clearly, a small carrier with a thin traffic base

Root brothers' SW1200 #2274 rolls toward the Mountain Fir mill on former Valley & Siletz trackage.

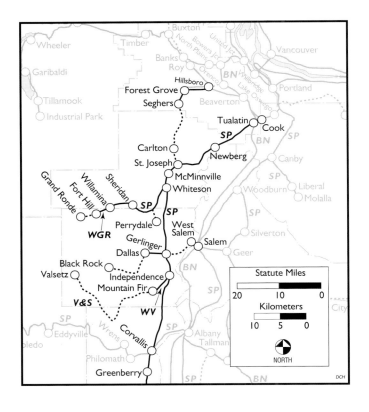

*Willamette Valley Railroad and the Willamina & Grand Ronde Railway,
with Southern Pacific connecting lines Willamina Branch, West Side Branch,
Dallas Branch, West Side-Seghers Branch, and Newberg Branch*

could not justify this measure of upkeep, and the line faced closure.

Relief came in 1981 and 1983, however, when hard cash grants came through to save the line. Credit for this reprieve should go to the U.S. Congress and its foresight in passage of two beneficial pieces of legislation. First came the "Railroad Revitalization and Regulatory Reform Act of 1976," providing federal grants to states for the purpose of preserving rail service on lines approved for abandonment by the ICC. Then came the "Local Rail Service Assistance Act of 1978," which expanded the program to ensure that grants could be used to upgrade light-density lines *prior* to abandonment. Both laws are important tools to help economically dependent communities preserve rail service.

The state of Oregon, however, added a further stipulation: perceived public benefits must exceed costs. Of course, there was a convoluted formula drawn up to reach a cost/benefit ratio, and at first this formula was *not* favorable to the Willamina & Grand Ronde. Consequently, in 1980, the state Department of Transportation had recommended against public investment to upgrade the WGR line—due to the supposed negative cost/benefit ratio.

As the trackage west of Fort Hill was generating little freight traffic, it was projected as not being worth the heavy financial investment for rehabilitation. Thus, nearly three miles of track beyond Fort Hill was abandoned in 1985. The state of Oregon relented on the remaining trackage, however, and the Willamina-Fort Hill segment was rescued by the new federal Local Rail Service Assistance grants. From 1981 to 1983, hundreds of ties were replaced, crushed rock was put down to provide solid ballast, and the light, worn rail along virtually the entire route was replaced with stronger 90-lb. rail. In addition, the track was resurfaced, and a bit of alignment

Above—July 19, 1990: the Santiam Branch Local, also known as the "BN Logger," rolls along rural environs near Weldwood, with five cars and a BN caboose behind GP9 #1875. Alongside the right-of-way are summer weeds and an antique whistle sign, symbols of Oregon's branchline network.

Right—Remnants of the Oregon Pacific Railroad's "Webfoot Route." These pilings once carried freight and passenger trains across the tidal flats between Toledo and Yaquina City. Now they are merely a ghostly tribute to Colonel Thomas Hogg's dream of making the Oregon Pacific a key transcontinental railroad.

Left—The buds on the trees are just beginning to explode into life in this view from Sheridan on April 2, 1990. The westbound Willamina Local rumbles onto a battered trestle over a nameless stream. The train, headed by two SD9s (#4370 and #4433 on this run), operates out of McMinnville six days a week to serve customers on the Willamina Branch and to interchange cars with the Willamina & Grand Ronde Railway. Southern Pacific, by way of the Willamina Branch, provides the W&GR with its sole connection to the outside world.

Above—The morning of February 15, 1990, finds the entire Willamette Valley enjoying a rare heavy snowfall. Rolling through Corvallis in an almost blinding snowstorm, the Toledo Hauler is being pulled by seven locomotives, including two TEBU slugs and SP GP40-2 #7950 on the point. The Toledo-bound freight bulls along the right-of-way that divides Sixth Street at a required 10 miles per hour in town.

Right—In October 1990, GP38-2 #2259 switches cars at the James River Corporation's huge paper mill at Halsey, on BN's Oregon Electric Branch.

Above—SP's Whiteson Turn crosses the bridge over the Willamette River at Menefee in the Autumn of 1992.

Above right—The Oregon Electric Branch feeds operations on several of BN's Oregon branchlines. On March 27, 1991, the BN Logger switches boxcars at a Willamette Industries mill in Foster, at the end of the Santiam Branch. Handling the day's chores is chopped-nose GP9 #1741.

Right—On May 9, 1990, an Oregon Coastline Express excursion train skims across Nehalem Bay with one car in tow, brightening the already spectacular scenery with its colorful striping. The Alco C415 locomotive is ex-Columbia & Cowlitz, the passenger car is ex-SP, and the former SP roadbed is now owned by the Port of Tillamook Bay Railroad. The excursion line's faithful Alco, accustomed to moving long cuts of flatcars loaded with logs, handles the task with ease.

Far right—The Spirit of Oregon, led by Alco C415s #701 and #702, at Banks, September 4, 1993.

Above—January 26, 1990: Willamette Valley Railroad's flagship locomotive, EMD SW1200 #201 (ex-SP #2273), brings five flatcar loads of lumber from the Mountain Fir Lumber Company, the shortline's lone customer, to V&S Junction. Later in the day, SP's Dallas Local will collect the cars and start them on their way to California. The line to the left is SP's West Side Branch; it sees service three days a week.

Left—WVRD #201 shuffles cars around the interchange yard at isolated V&S Junction on April 6, 1990, as apple trees blossom alongside. This three-track yard and a 1.9-mile line to Mountain Fir is all that remains of the 41-mile Valley & Siletz Railroad.

Right—Drain, on SP's Siskiyou Branch, sees a northbound freight headed by SP SD40T-2 #8524 rolling toward Eugene, July 27, 1993.

*Above—Willamette &
Pacific's McMinnville
Hauler is westbound at
Lake Oswego, July 5, 1993.*

*Left—An SP freight is
northbound on SP's Siskiyou
Line, nearing Cottage
Grove, July 27, 1993.*

work performed. In all, some $450,000 was invested to insure the continued viability of the line.

Currently, the WGR operates 5.2 miles of track, straddling the line between Polk and Yamhill counties while following the Yamhill River to Fort Hill. At Fort Hill is the WGR's primary customer: the Fort Hill Lumber Company sawmill, part of the Hampton Lumber chain. Fort Hill Lumber normally ships between five to eight flatcar loads of mostly California bound lumber each week, although by mid-1990, rail shipments fell substantially owing to log shortages. Consequently, continued long-term operation of the line is uncertain.

The railway also serves the Morton Alder Company in Willamina, shipping a boxcar or two every month packed with alderwood 2x4s and 2x6s. Morton Alder Company has no rail spur, so when it needs a boxcar, it's simply left on the WGR's main track for loading, then is picked up the next time a train comes along on its way to Fort Hill.

The Willamina & Grand Ronde's motive power includes an ex-SP SW1200 (WGR #2274) still in weathered SP paint, but with the Southern Pacific name painted over. Also on the roster is an ex-LP&N Alco S2 (WGR #110), built in 1945. The orange Alco isn't often used, but is ready to go if needed. These units have no roundhouse or train shed; they're out in the elements constantly, resting in a yard in Willamina or on a siding in Fort Hill when not in use.

Southern Pacific operates a six-days-per-week local out of McMinnville—the Willamina Local—that connects with the WGR. It's usually powered by a pair of SD9s, which seem to be everywhere on SP's

Above top—The Dallas Local arrives at Corvallis Junction, where the West Side Branch meets the Toledo Branch. It has traveled up the valley to Independence and along the Dallas Branch to a Willamette Industries sawmill at the railhead in Dallas. Corvallis is home base for this thrice-weekly train that provides interchange with the Independence-based Willamette Valley Railroad. SD9 #4411 is in charge; the date is April 11, 1990.

Above—Willamina & Grand Ronde Railway's aging Alco S2, built in December 1945, is understandably showing a bit of rust. Regardless, this venerable ex-Longview, Portland & Northern workhorse is stored in serviceable condition in the joint WGR/SP yard at Willamina, where the WGR's 5.2 miles of track begin.

Left—The battle-scarred builder's plate for WGR #110.

Locomotive Rosters*
Willamina & Grand Ronde Railway

WGR #2274, EMD SW1200 (ex-SP #2274, built 1965)
WGR #110, Alco S2 (ex-LP&N, built 1945)

Willamette Valley Railroad

WVRD #201, EMD SW1200 (ex-SP #2273, built 1965)
WVRD #2890, EMD GP9 (ex-SP, built 1959; out of service)

*Note: These locomotives are essentially under the same owner-ship and are subject to rotating operating assignments. This roster reflects which carrier normally used the units between 1989-1992. While this book was in preparation, the Root brothers negotiated the purchase of additional engines: ex-SP SD9 #4433 and ex-SP GP9 #3859.

Willamina Branch (SP)
Stations

Whiteson	MP 730.6
Winch	MP 737.2
Broadmead	MP 737.7
Ballston	MP 740.5
Sheridan	MP 744.7
Shipley	MP 746.3
Willamina	MP 749.3
End of branch	MP 749.5

Newberg Branch (SP)
Direct Traffic Control Blocks

Newberg Block	West MP 748.4; East MP 748.1
Sherwood Block	West MP 748.1; East MP 757.5
Tualatin Block	West MP 757.5; East MP 764.0

Newberg Branch (SP)
Stations

Cook	MP 764.0
Tualatin	MP 762.0
Cipole	MP 759.5
Sherwood	MP 757.6
Rex	MP 753.0
Springbrook	MP 750.8
Newberg	MP 748.5
Dundee	MP 746.1
Dayton	MP 742.1
St. Joseph	MP 738.0

backwoods mileage. The local serves several customers along the 18.7-mile Willamina Branch (from Whiteson, on the West Side Branch 4.2 miles south of McMinnville, to Willamina). Major shippers on this SP branch include Willamina Lumber Company and Taylor Lumber Company, both in Willamina, and West Valley Farmers in Sheridan. Freight cars reaching this branch are handled over Southern Pacific's Newberg Branch, basically the Willamina & Grand Ronde's sole remaining connection to the outside world. The Newberg Branch runs from Cook, near Lake Grove, to St. Joseph, about three miles north of McMinnville. The 26-mile line serves about a dozen firms, with a Smurfit Corporation paper mill in Newberg being the major shipper.

The Newberg Branch also provides access to several West Side Branch customers south of a 12.7-mile segment of West Side trackage (Carlton-Seghers) abandoned in 1985. Chief among these is Cascade Steel Rolling Mills, Inc., at McMinnville. Six days a week, the "Steel Train"—better known as the Whiteson Turn—hauls gondolas filled with scrap metal to the huge facility. Cascade Steel is doubling the capacity of its plant to as much as 700,000 tons a year, the result of a $35 million investment featuring construction of a 12-story tall "melt shop"—a scrap-melting furnace. This is great news for SP and for the local economy. The mill employs more than 400 people, and, with the expansion, is being billed as the largest steel recycler on the West Coast.

McMinnville, once a key station on the West Side Branch, now is somewhat isolated due to abandonments of segments of the West Side Branch. All rail traffic outbound from McMinnville now goes by way of the Newberg Branch. As a result, the Newberg Branch should be in line for some accelerated track maintenance. Yet rumors persist that SP is planning to reactivate the Derry-Amity (MP 715.0 to MP 728.1) portion of the West Side Branch in order to improve service to McMinnville—something of a boom station for SP primarily due to Cascade Steel's expansion.

Intriguingly, SP ran several "Derry Turn" trains in June 1991 to pull surplus freight cars off the West Side Branch between Derry and Amity—possibly in preparation for the reopening of the West Side route. On June 11, 1991, for example, three SD9s, led by SP

The Grand Ronde depot on the Longview, Portland & Northern as it appeared in the mid-1960s. This line from Grand Ronde to Willamina became the Willamina & Grand Ronde Railway in 1980.
Photo: Jack Holst, Collection of PNWC—NRHS.

#4352, hauled 128 deadlined cars, almost entirely boxcars, back to Eugene. Some of these cars have been sold to shortline carriers; the remainder are to be scrapped.

Opening this segment would ease SP's problems in moving heavy-tonnage trains over Rex Hill on the Newberg Branch, while allowing agricultural shippers along the route to receive direct service. And the reopening would expedite the movement of goods to the south, by allowing the routing of trains through Albany and Eugene instead of Portland.

Currently, the Whiteson Turn leaves Portland's 100-acre Brooklyn Yard in late afternoon, and reaches McMinnville several hours later. The Portland-bound Whiteson Turn waits for cars being ferried off the Willamina Branch, including whatever the WGR has passed off to SP at Willamina, before heading back to Brooklyn Yard on a moonlight run. The train is scheduled for duty Sunday through Friday. Typical consists of McMinnville-bound trains are mixed: flatcars, boxcars, covered hoppers, tank cars, and, above all, gondolas—a few empty but most loaded with scrap metal. Meanwhile, Newberg's Smurfit Corporation paper mill rates its own all-boxcar train—the Newberg Turn—six days per week, Monday through Saturday. The boxcars carry scrap paper to feed the mill. Multiple SD9s, with an occasional GP9 thrown in, power virtually all movements over the line; rarely is any other type of locomotive seen.

The Newberg Branch remains in solid condition. It is FRA Class 2, permitting operation at up to 25 mph. Reflecting the importance SP places on servicing Cascade Steel, the line is well-kept, with crushed rock and 90-lb. rail predominating.

Roughly 20 miles southeast of Willamina, in Independence, the Willamette Valley Railroad (WVRD) was formed out of the remains of the Valley & Siletz Railroad. Opened in 1916, the Valley & Siletz ran southwest from Independence to the town of Valsetz. At its peak, and for most of its history, the line was 40.6 miles long. Valsetz was a classic railroad

Above—SP's Whiteson Turn passes through Lake Oswego in January 1993 as it heads Portland-bound with four SD9s. The building on the right is the former "Red Electric" substation.

Left—The Newberg Turn, with SP SD9 #4416 in the lead, crosses Rex Hill trestle on its return to Portland, June 27, 1991.

Right—The Willamina Local, the WGR's rail connection to the outside world, rolls through Sheridan, April 2, 1990. Two SD9s, #4370 and #4433, take this train as far as Willamina before returning to McMinnville to pass their cars on to the nightly Whiteson Turn, bound for Portland.

and lumber company town. Even the name "Valsetz" was merely a contraction of the name of the railway that served it. Wood products and the railroad were so essential to the community that when Boise Cascade finally departed, the town soon literally ceased to exist.

Boise Cascade used the railroad to haul lumber and logs between two of its mills in Valsetz and Independence until June 1978, before paring operations back to Pedee, a small town 17 miles from Independence. By the end of 1979, only three miles of track remained in service: between V&S Junction (Independence) and Stapleton, at MP 3.12. Finally, on January 2, 1985, the Willamette Valley Railroad bought approximately two miles of the Valley & Siletz trackage—V&S Junction to Mountain Fir—and Boise Cascade got out of the railroad business in Oregon. The surviving segment extends from a small, three-track interchange yard (it once held five tracks, but two tracks have been removed) just north of Independence, and terminates at the Mountain Fir Lumber Company located at MP 1.87. All remaining

trackage west of the Mountain Fir mill was abandoned by April 1985.

In actuality, the line was little more than a spur to the lumber mill in recent years; there were no other shippers. Mountain Fir had been providing as many as seven or eight carloads of outbound lumber each week, but in May 1992, the Mountain Fir mill closed, and the line fell dormant. Boise Cascade continues to operate a mill at Independence and the tracks pass directly alongside the facility, but Boise Cascade does not ship any products by rail and is not a customer of the Willamette Valley.

What's left of the former Valley & Siletz trackage is still in fairly good shape: 75-lb. rail, ties fair, mostly crushed rock for ballast. But for now it will be used only for car storage, unless another firm leases the Mountain Fir property and reopens the mill at the end of the line. Following the closure of the Mountain Fir mill, the Roots decided to move their headquarters to McMinnville, close to the Willamina & Grand Ronde line.

For now, all that's left of the Willamette Valley

West Side Branch (SP)
Direct Traffic Control Blocks

Wellsdale Block .... West MP 691.0; East MP 699.2
Independence Block .... West MP 699.2; East MP 709.0
Derry Block .... West MP 709.0; East MP 715.0
McCoy Block .... West MP 715.0; East MP 722.8
Amity Block .... West MP 722.8; East MP 730.0

Valley & Siletz Railroad
Stations

Independence
Stapleton
Neahr
Helmick
Mitchell
Simpson
Crisp
Tartar
Wallinch
Pedee
Ritner
Kings Valley
Tiff
Hoskins
Kopplein
Arell
Seekay
Valsetz

Railroad's operations is a freight car repair business. Supplemental revenue has been generated by subcontracting with Gunderson, Inc., a freight car designer and builder based in Portland, to complete minor upgrades and/or repairs on an assortment of cars. Orders for Ventura County Railway boxcars, Washington Central gondolas, and Coe Rail trailer-flats have been handled in the early 1990s. This work is performed in Independence, at the WVRD engine house. Locomotives can also be repaired there, including units from other shortlines in the region. For example, a Port of Tillamook Bay SD9—POTB #4414—was worked on there in 1991.

A Southern Pacific freight called the Dallas Local, coming through Independence on Mondays, Wednesdays, and Fridays, used to pick up and set out cars for the Willamette Valley when the mill was in business. Exchanged cars were primarily 53-ft. flatcars

and 60-ft. bulkhead flats. Many of the bulkhead flats sported WGR reporting marks; these were usually ex-ICG cars.

The SP's Dallas Local continues to operate out of Corvallis with an SD9 and works through to an agricultural complex at Derry, about 26 miles north of Corvallis (customers include Derry Warehouse Company and Willamette Seed Company) before heading west toward Dallas. North of Derry, and continuing as far as Amity—13.1 miles—the West Side Branch is being used for storage of surplus rolling stock. Shippers in Amity are handled by the Willamina Local.

In Dallas, a Willamette Industries sawmill sits at the end of the 5.3-mile Dallas Branch, which is accessed via a wye at Gerlinger Junction on the connecting West Side Branch. The 10 mph, east-west Dallas branchline now remains in place only from Dallas to Thielsen. The line once ran another 10 miles east from Thielsen to Salem, before removal of most of this trackage in the late 1970s. (At the far western end of the line, an extension to Black Rock, about 13 miles west of Dallas, was abandoned in the 1960s.) The Dallas Local crew switches boxcars and flatcars at the Willamette Industries mill and returns to Corvallis, stopping as needed to pull a loaded flatcar or two from the Marys River Lumber Company mill at Lewisburg, four miles north of Corvallis.

Until the early 1980s, SP operated a daily train out of Eugene called the "West Sider." This train served customers along the West Side Branch between Corvallis Junction and Hillsboro, terminating at Brooklyn Yard. V&S Junction was always a key station on this train's route, with bright green and white boxcars (Boise Cascade and V&S Railroad colors) being set out and loads picked up. But after SP abandoned a short section of the train's route between Carlton and Seghers, the West Sider could run no more.

All connecting service for V&S Junction and the Willamette Valley Railroad is now provided exclusively by the thrice-weekly Dallas Local, while a Stimson Timber mill at Seghers, at the end of the West Side-Seghers Branch, is supplied with cars three days a week by a train crew operating from Hillsboro. The West Side-Seghers Branch begins in Hillsboro at MP 765.3 and terminates at the Stimson mill at MP

Above—SW1200 #2274 switches the Mountain Fir lumber mill near Independence in June 1991. The flatcar will be left at the junction for the Southern Pacific to pick up.

Left—Valley & Siletz #7 rests at Independence along with V&S caboose #303, June 1968.
Photo: Jack Holst, Collection of PNWC—NRHS.

An increasingly rare handful of "Kodachrome" units still spice up operations on SP's Oregon branchlines. In March 1991, SP SD9 #4363, heading the Dallas Local, is working on the pleasingly-rural West Side Branch directly north of Derry. The train is placing a cut of D&RGW boxcars into storage, as the West Side Branch is blocked with hundreds of surplus cars between Derry and Amity.

757.0. Directly south of the line into Seghers is the abandoned roadbed of former West Side Branch trackage that, until 1985, continued on via Yamhill and Carlton. Another remnant of the West Side Branch—extending south from Carlton to St. Joseph, 4.2 miles—survived for a few years after 1985, but was eventually taken out of service. The line was used for storage for awhile, then removed in 1992.

The Willamette Valley's locomotive roster comprises two units: an SW1200 and a GP9. SW1200 #201 is ex-SP #2273 (interestingly enough, WGR's SW1200 is ex-SP #2274, yet the consecutive numbers are apparently pure coincidence), and has been painted in red and orange "Daylight" colors. Another former SP unit, still in SP gray and red, is GP9 #2890. This unit is stored out-of-service in front of the effi-

cient two-stall train shed that Boise Cascade built in 1977, shortly before the company quit the line. Also stored inside the Independence train shed is a non-operating ex-Santa Maria Valley steamer, a 2-6-2. Both of the WGR/WVRD SW1200s have proven especially reliable. SP completed major servicing on both switcher units in 1981—even putting on new wheels—before placing them in storage in 1982 when business slowed. As a result, they remain in prime condition under the Roots' ownership.

Until the closure of the Mountain Fir mill, scheduling of WVRD/WGR trains typically worked like this: on Mondays, Wednesdays, and Fridays, a train crew began the day in Independence, switched at the Mountain Fir facility, and carried loaded cars back to V&S Junction for interchange with the Southern

Pacific. After noon, the same crew drove north to Willamina, fired up workhorse engine WGR #2274, and took empties to Fort Hill. After switching out the mill, the train returned to Willamina with the day's loads, where they are handed over to SP.

Of course, the WVRD and WGR schedules were dependent upon the needs of the mills. As is often the case with ever-responsive shortlines, they worked extra hours to please customers and alleviate problems caused by a sometimes unpredictable flow of empty cars from SP. Car supply has been a problem at times for WVRD/WGR shippers. Otherwise, on Tuesdays and Thursdays, if the shortlines were not hauling freight, the staff took time to "fix everything," in the words of George Lavacot.

The Willamina & Grand Ronde was merged into the Willamette Valley on March 10, 1986, and the WGR briefly ceased to exist as a separate business entity. Instead of the Willamette Valley Railroad and the Willamina & Grand Ronde Railway, the lines became the Willamette Valley Railroad—Mountain Fir Branch (also known for awhile as "V&S Branch"); and Willamette Valley Railroad—Fort Hill Branch (also known as "W&GR Branch"). This is essentially how they exist today, yet for business reasons they "unmerged" in 1988. Although continuing under the same ownership, they are again regarded as separate railroads. Both shortlines operate on Federal Railroad Administration "Excepted" track, which permits a maximum train speed of 10 mph. But, given the limited number of miles served by these roads, a 10 mph limit cannot be considered a serious impediment to the timely transfer of goods.

In 1986, the Southern Pacific branchlines connecting with the Roots' two shortlines were categorized by the Oregon Public Utility Commission as being in "Questionable" status, meaning they were likely candidates for abandonment. In fact, another line that connected with the Willamina Branch at Broadmead—the Perrydale Branch—was removed in 1985 (this branchline went 2.2 miles south from Broadmead to service Elliott Feed & Seed in Perrydale). Yet the entire Willamina Branch (MP 730.6 to MP 749.5), along with the West Side Branch from Corvallis Junction to McMinnville (MP 689.9 to MP 734.9), are both considered by the OPUC as mileage that "appears to have sufficient

Dallas Branch (SP)
Stations

Thielsen	MP 728.5
Gerlinger	MP 728.9
Dallas	MP 733.8

West Side-Seghers Branch (SP)
Stations

Hillsboro	MP 765.3
Cornelius	MP 761.7
Carnation	MP 759.2
Seghers	MP 754.9
Stimson-Forest Fiber	MP 757.0

Willamette Valley Railroad's ghostly ex-SP GP9 #2890 rests forlornly alongside WVRD headquarters in Independence, June 1991.

traffic to warrant continued operation, but the present carrier has indicated an interest in disposing of the line."

The Roots, however, have shown interest in expanding if Southern Pacific sells any of its adjoining branchlines. It wouldn't take too much trackage for the WVRD/WGR owners to be able to join their disconnected shortlines. There is significant traffic on the two SP lines, and both are in reasonably good condition. The Willamina Branch is built with 80-lb. rail and is in FRA Class 2 condition, allowing speeds

Carload Figures
Willamette Valley Railroad (WVRD)—

1986: 402
1987: 896 (includes shipments on the WGR)
1988: 394 (after "unmerging")

Willamina & Grand Ronde Railway (WGR)—

1986: 727
1987: 896 (combined with WVRD figures)
1988: 344 (after "unmerging")

of up to 25 mph, while much of the West Side Branch is in even better shape. Between Corvallis Junction and Independence, for example, the branchline is built with 132-lb. continuous welded rail. Ties are in excellent shape, and the ballast is crushed rock. As a result, this section of track is rated in Class 3 condition, permitting 40 mph operation.

A proposed sale of the WGR to the Fort Hill Lumber Company, and operating it as a spur track off SP's Willamina Branch, no longer seems likely. Of more concern is the fact that both the Willamette Valley and the Willamina & Grand Ronde are considered "Endangered" (translation: "Line does not appear secure for five years") by the Oregon PUC.

A major reason for this bleak outlook has been the loss of some commercial business as shippers move materials by truck to Union Pacific and Burlington Northern reload sites to take advantage of single-line rates. However, SP has adopted more competitive rates for Oregon lumber products, and some traffic has been recaptured. A strong Southern Pacific system is essential to both the WVRD and WGR.

The Roots have carved out a small niche in Oregon's transportation network. The Willamette Valley Railroad and the Willamina & Grand Ronde Railway have been in existence for only a few years, and the next several years in their history should be especially telling. From potential expansion to abandonment, anything still appears possible for these evolving shortlines. 🔫

SP's Dallas Local arrives at the three-track interchange yard at V&S Junction on the morning of March 27, 1991, leaving a few flatcars for the Willamette Valley Railroad to collect. When the Dallas Local returns from its duties in Dallas, a couple of loaded flats will be waiting; these cars will be hauled to Corvallis. This train operates from Corvallis to Dallas and back three days a week. SP SD9 #4363 is working this day's run.

CHAPTER 8
SEMAPHORES AND TIMBER

Southern Pacific's Siskiyou Line and White City Branch,
with shortline connections Yreka Western Railroad, WCTU Railway,
and Oregon, Pacific & Eastern Railway

Siskiyou. In Plains Cree, it means "spotted horse" or "packhorse," and this Indian name reportedly came to be identified with the mountains when Archibald R. McLeod of the Hudson's Bay Company led a pack string across the range in 1828. (At the time, Canadians held a hegemony over the Pacific Northwest fur trade.) A brutal snowstorm left many pack animals dead, including a prized bobtail racehorse. As the story goes, McLeod's French-Canadian and Indian followers applied the name "Siskiyou" to the mountain pass where they'd encountered the storm, and subsequently the Indian word was applied to the entire mountain range. Many decades later, Southern Pacific Railroad chose to name its new north-south mainline after the rugged, mountainous terrain it crossed.

On December 17, 1887, the Oregon & California Railroad completed construction of its Portland-San Francisco mainline. Two sections of track—one coming south from Portland, the other built north from San Francisco—joined at Ashland, Oregon. It was a tremendous day in the history of Oregon transportation. For the first time, Oregon goods could be moved directly to San Francisco and Oakland, and dozens of dignitaries and newspaper reporters converged on Ashland to record the momentous event.

About all that remains of those glory days is a bronze plaque marking the site where the new line was ceremoniously joined with a traditional golden spike. Today, the humble memorial remains all-but-forgotten in a tiny park adjacent to the Southern

Pacific freight yard in Ashland, but the text explains the importance of the opening of this right-of-way:

> On December 17, 1887, Charles Crocker drove the Golden Spike in the rail yard just south of this point, connecting the Oregon & California tracks from the north with those of the California & Oregon, now the Southern Pacific, from the south. This action opened the Pacific Northwest to California and the Southwest, completing a circle of railroads around the United States.

Passenger trains started operating on the "Siskiyou Route" immediately. Logically enough, the "Oregon Express" was the name of the primary northbound train on the Siskiyou Line, while the "California Express" headed south. Passenger trains operated continuously between Portland and Ashland from December 17, 1887, until August 7, 1955.

Southern Pacific's Siskiyou Line officially begins at Springfield Junction (MP 644.3) on the Cascade Line a few miles east of Eugene Yard. From there, the track runs south precisely 300.3 miles through Roseburg, Grants Pass, Ashland, and all the way to Black Butte, California (MP 344.0). At Black Butte it rejoins SP's Shasta Line between Klamath Falls, Oregon, and Dunsmuir, California.

For nearly four decades, the Siskiyou route—SP's mainline—was the key rail link connecting Oregon and California. However, it lost much of its prestige when the "Natron Cutoff" project opened the Cascade Line on August 7, 1926. This newer route funnelled north-south trains via Klamath Falls instead of Ashland, and from that day forward the Siskiyou Line was relegated to "secondary" status.

A Southern Pacific train led by F-unit #627 heads
southbound at Glendale in January 1969.
Photo: Fred Smith, Collection of Tom Dill.

A Southern Pacific passenger train stopped at the Medford depot in February 1952. The train is headed southbound toward the Siskiyous with locomotive #2407 on the lead.
Photo: W.C. Whittaker, Collection of Tom Dill.

The "Cascade Route" is roughly 25 miles shorter than the Siskiyou Line, and, more significantly, has fewer curves and easier grades. Now, almost all bridge traffic rides the Cascade Line, with primarily local cars, or occasional outbound empties, traveling the Siskiyou Subdivision.

The Siskiyou Line was built well, and over the entire right-of-way the track has been maintained at a relatively high standard: 132-lb. rail predominates, although in spots there is 90-lb. and 110-lb., as well as some 136-lb. Ballast along the line is mostly crushed rock, except for the segment between Ashland and Black Butte, which is mostly cinders—commonplace in volcano country.

Much of the track is rated as FRA Class 3, meaning it is considered safe for trains running up to 40 mph. Between Grants Pass and Ashland (45 miles) and between Eugene and Divide (26 miles), it is Class 3. The remainder is FRA Class 2, rated for a maximum of 25 mph.

Despite the line's generous federal speed advisories, actual operating speeds are limited not by roadbed conditions but by the route's grades and tight curves. Moreover, several narrow tunnels demand a reduced speed limit. Due to restricted clearance, these tunnels also keep "Plate F" cars, primarily woodchip haulers, off segments of the route.

The Siskiyou Line serves Oregon's most productive timber region, and as a result the line's continued viability is considered vital to the state's economy. How vital? Consider that in 1988, Oregon Public Utility Commission figures revealed that 70,000 revenue shipments (definition: *loads*) were handled on the Siskiyou Line. Obviously, a tremendous volume is being moved over this secondary track. To put this in clearer perspective, the Denver & Rio Grande Western's application to purchase SP stated that about 80,000 carloads of wood products originate on SP's Oregon rail network annually. If D&RGW's figure is accurate, then nearly

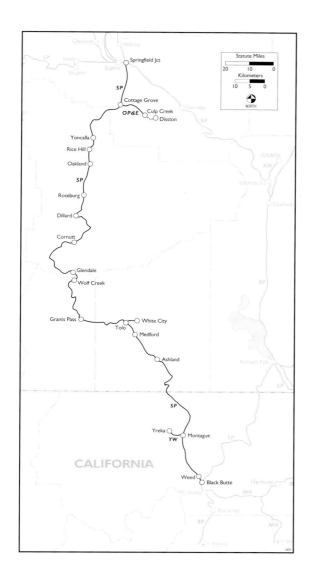

Southern Pacific's Siskiyou Line and White City Branch,
with shortline connections Yreka Western Railroad, WCTU Railway,
and Oregon, Pacific & Eastern Railway

seven-eighths of SP's Oregon lumber traffic comes directly off the Siskiyou Line. Furthermore, many industry observers believe that traffic over the Siskiyou Subdivision could significantly increase if SP's sales managers aggressively pursued woodchip customers. Yet SP has all but turned woodchip hauling over to truckers because it's not an "expensive ticket" item.

Despite its clear domination, lumber has not been the only commodity moving along this line in recent years. At Riddle, Glenbrook Nickel has opened a mining operation at the former Hanna Nickel facility, and the station is again moving goods by rail. And just outside of Springfield Junction on Siskiyou trackage, there is a plastics firm that manufactures an assortment of durable PVC pipes. Two hundred miles to the south, in Medford and the surrounding area, loads of fruit—primarily pears, often packaged in gift boxes—move out in Pacific Fruit Express refrigerator cars. This traffic is especially heavy in the autumn.

Siskiyou Line (SP)
Stations

Numerous lumber companies are situated here and there at different stations alongside the meandering tracks. All told, there are about 30 lumber shippers on the line. This provides enough business along the way to warrant the positioning of local switchers in Roseburg, Grants Pass, and Medford.

The busiest customer is Roseburg Forest Products Company, the largest private timber business in Oregon. Based in Roseburg, it weighs in as the heaviest shipper of forest products on SP nationwide, which is quite a distinction. Roseburg Forest Products raked in over $500 million in revenues in 1992. Fifty cars a day go out from its extensive complex of Douglas County mills, and SP has a local crew assigned to handle the load six days a week. It's easy to understand why dedicated train service is required when one realizes what is included under the Roseburg Forest Products Company's umbrella. In addition to a plywood mill in Roseburg, there are several different operations in Dillard, about 10 miles south of Roseburg: i.e., two plywood mills, a lumber mill, a plywood remanufacturing plant, and a particleboard facility. There is also a veneer mill in Dixonville, roughly five miles north of Roseburg.

Recent news from some other firms along the line promises to add to SP's traffic volume. In March 1990, Willamette Industries agreed to lease and operate a laminated veneer mill that was closing in Winston, not far from Roseburg; and Oregon Fir Millwork announced plans to purchase a mill in White City, hiring as many as 100 new employees to manufacture wooden mouldings. And an aluminum company, Alcan, has opened a facility in Wilbur, nine miles north of Roseburg.

A description of this "backwater mainline" in the 1990s is a tale of a diverse, frantic schedule of freight service. As many as 11 different trains might work along the Siskiyou Subdivision on any given day, in a crazy-quilt, forever changing pattern. In early 1993, there were two through trains on the line that had maintained a fairly consistent schedule in recent years. Six days a week, a train runs between Eugene Yard and Medford to gather loads and maintain the flow of empties to local crews working the line. (Medford, a key station on the Siskiyou Line, is about 208 miles from Eugene.) A second through freight is designed to move cars between Eugene and Roseburg,

Above—Heavy road units, including brand new Cotton Belt GP60 #9666 and SP SD45T-2 #9316, at Walker in July 1991 on SP's Siskiyou Line. The units on the left will be attached as helpers on a southbound train to Medford.

Left—At Goshen, SP SD40T-2 #8321 powers a long freight southbound to Medford (westbound by timetable).

The White City Branch leaves the Siskiyou Line at Tolo. Here, in this early 1980s photo, SP SD9 #4402 heads toward White City.

Photo: Ed Austin, Collection of Tom Dill.

a distance of approximately 75 miles. This operation, as with the Eugene-Medford train, also rolls six days per week. Trains in the opposite direction—Medford to Eugene and Roseburg to Eugene—also operate six days a week.

Until August 1992, a third train—a manifest freight out of Roseville, California—ran through to Medford seven days a week. But with carloads out of southern Oregon dwindling, SP officials decided to halt through train service between Ashland and Black Butte, California. Freight cars will instead be hauled north to Eugene before being sent south on the Cascade Line via Klamath Falls. The diversion adds a day or two to transit times for goods moving from southern Oregon to California markets, but SP managers have been quick to point out that this is not a prelude to abandonment of the line.

"It's still viable," says Mike Healy, manager of field operations for SP in Eugene. "It's an outlet should we need it."

There is a variety of motive power pulling long

haul trains on the Siskiyou Line. SD9s, GP9s, SD40s, SD40T-2s, SD45s, and SD45T-2s predominate, but B40-8s and even GP60s make appearances. Pool locomotives (including units from the Union Pacific, Denver & Rio Grande Western, and Burlington Northern) are seen now and then.

Local service is much more elaborate, with nine different trains normally operating on weekdays. Alterations in schedules are not uncommon, but one thing has remained consistent in recent years: invariably, local trains move with SD9s on the point. Basically, local operations are arranged as follows: from Eugene Yard, where all Siskiyou Line southbounds originate, there is a train known as the Yoncalla Local that works six days per week. Yoncalla is a small town located about 40 miles south of Eugene. Despite the name, there are no shippers in Yoncalla any more, due to the closure of a lumber mill there years ago. The crew normally serves the big North Douglas Wood Products plywood mill (formerly owned by Bohemia) in Drain, about five miles north of Yoncalla, and interchanges with the Oregon, Pacific & Eastern Railway at Cottage Grove. The Yoncalla Local is also charged with switching an industrial district at Springfield, on the Cascade Line, a little over a mile east (west by timetable) of Springfield Junction.

Looking further south, there are three local crews based out of Roseburg. One crew runs north to Oakland and back (17 miles one way) with a local train romantically referred to as the "Rice Hill Rocket." Another crew heads south as far as Riddle (28 miles), serving shippers in Myrtle Creek and Riddle. Both trains are scheduled five days a week. Also, the Dillard Turn runs to Dillard six days per week. In Dillard, the crew sets out empties at Roseburg Forest Products' mills and returns to Roseburg with the day's lumber loads.

Grants Pass has a local crew on duty five days a week. A switching crew there takes the Glendale Turn to mills in Merlin and Glendale, about 34 miles north of Grants Pass.

Medford is home base to three crews, all of which work local turns five days a week. The White City Local works north through Central Point—a relatively busy mill town—then continues to the junction of the White City Branch at Tolo. From Tolo, trains roll east for five miles to White City, where cars are interchanged with the shortline WCTU Railway. Another local goes north from Medford to Rogue River, 23 miles. A third train runs south 13 miles to reach shippers in Phoenix, Talent, and Ashland.

Finally, at the southern end of the line, a crew based out of Dunsmuir, California (Dunsmuir is located on the Shasta Line at MP 322.1, about 22 miles south of where the Siskiyou Branch begins at Black Butte), serves Siskiyou Branch shippers in Weed and Montague, California. This train, known as the Montague Local, also provides interchange with the McCloud River Railroad (at Mount Shasta, south of Black Butte) and the Yreka Western Railroad (at Montague).

South of Ashland, helper units have almost always been necessary on long trains working the steep grades on the slopes of 7,530-foot Mount Ashland, the highest peak in the Siskiyou Range. Until the suspension of through service south of Ashland, helpers congregated in Dunsmuir to the south and

A rock slide temporarily closed the Siskiyou Line near Tolo in 1964.

Photo: Southern Pacific Transportation Co., Collection of Tom Dill.

Siskiyou Branch (SP)
Direct Traffic Control Blocks

Gazelle Block	West MP 360.8; East MP 361.9
Montague Block	West MP 361.9; East MP 375.7
Hornbrook Block	West MP 375.7; East MP 393.4
Siskiyou Block	West MP 393.4; East MP 412.8
Belleview Block	West MP 412.8; East MP 425.8
Talent Block	West MP 425.8; East MP 438.7
Central Point Block	West MP 444.5; East MP 450.6
Rogue River Block	West MP 450.6; East MP 471.0
Grants Pass Block	West MP 471.0; East MP 475.0
Hugo Block	West MP 475.0; East MP 488.1
Wolf Creek Block	West MP 488.1; East MP 506.1
Glendale Block	West MP 506.1; East MP 508.9
Cow Creek Block	West MP 508.9; East MP 539.0
Cornutt Block	West MP 539.0; East MP 541.7
Riddle Block	West MP 541.7; East MP 546.4
Dole Block	West MP 546.4; East MP 558.7
Green Block	West MP 563.0; East MP 571.0
Sutherlin Block	West MP 574.2; East MP 587.0
Rice Hill Block	West MP 587.0; East MP 597.6
Yoncalla Block	West MP 597.6; East MP 604.1
Divide Block	West MP 604.1; East MP 622.5
Cottage Grove Block	West MP 622.5; East MP 631.3
Goshen Block	West MP 631.3; East MP 642.0
Springfield Block	West MP 642.0; East MP 644.6

Kicking up dust as it races through Cottage Grove, a Eugene-bound freight powers along the northern end of the Siskiyou Line in July 1993. SD40T-2 #8524 leads the way.

Ashland or Medford to the north. For northbound trains, units were normally added in Dunsmuir or Black Butte. Although helper locomotives are commonly used north of Roseburg and in the mountains around Grants Pass, nowhere are gradients as severe as those found along the Oregon-California border. The grade at Tunnel 13, just beyond Siskiyou, is the steepest SP track anywhere: 3.67 percent. And Siskiyou Summit also is the line's highest elevation: 4,135 feet. There are 16 tunnels on the line, with the longest—Tunnel #13—being 3,108 feet long. From Siskiyou Summit, moving north, the roadbed descends 2,234 feet in 17 miles to reach the floor of the Rogue Valley near Ashland.

Ashland, a sleepy college town and home to a classy Shakespearean festival, was once a major player in SP's Siskiyou Line operations. The station, at MP 429.1, also served as a crew-change point. The last significant Oregon city before reaching the California border, Ashland lies roughly halfway between Portland and San Francisco, and thus developed into a key hub of rail activity. As recently as the late 1970s, SP invested in the construction of new fueling and sanding racks for the locomotives that constantly idled there. In recent years, however, SP has downgraded its presence in Ashland dramatically. No longer do crews take rest there; no longer is the depot open around the clock; no longer are heavy road locomotives heard purring at all times of the day or night.

The Ashland depot was closed, boarded up, and finally removed, and the motel rooms that SP built to accommodate train crews were razed. The new (and expensive) fueling racks were removed in 1989. What's left of Ashland Yard—most of the tracks have now been taken up—is used primarily for boxcar storage. The remaining customers in the area are handled by trains from Medford.

The Siskiyou Line is one of the few remaining major rail lines using semaphore signal towers. Unfortunately, but predictably, the semaphore towers are endangered and not likely to survive much longer. Southern Pacific has requested permission from the ICC to remove them from some 255 miles of Siskiyou trackage, citing their age. (Semaphores on SP's "Golden State Route" between El Paso, Texas, and Tucumcari, New Mexico, were taken down in 1988, although in that case they were replaced with modern signals.) Specifically, SP would like to pull its block signals between Gazelle, California (MP 360.8), and Glendale, Oregon (MP 509.8); and between Cornutt, Oregon (MP 538.8), and Springfield Junction (MP 644.4).

SP claims that it would cost $2.7 million to replace or repair 372 signals—some are three-quarters of a century old—in order to upgrade the anachronistic system. SP also estimates a savings of nearly half a million dollars annually if allowed to dismantle the aging equipment. These savings would be passed on to shippers, according to SP officials. In any case, SP argues that the signals are not necessary any more, citing statistics suggesting that more than 90 percent of rail/safety defects are not caught by the signaling network anyway. Nevertheless, in a meeting with the ICC and shipper groups, protests were voiced, citing safety and economic concerns.

The state of Oregon's presentation was delivered by David Astle, assistant commissioner of transportation for the Oregon PUC. Astle pointed out not only the economic importance of the line, but also, eruditely, that trains on the line often toil in severe weather conditions, including heavy rain, snow, and fog. The extremely long trains normally working the line tend to tie up automobile traffic as it is, Astle argued. But when train crews must operate without

SP's Ashland roundhouse as it appeared in August 1957. The brick structure was torn down shortly afterward, and the turntable was removed after being damaged in 1976.

Photo: Dave Clune, Collection of Tom Dill.

"Restricted speed," defined in *SP Western Region Timetable*

A speed that will permit stopping within one-half the range of vision; short of train, engine, railroad car, stop signal, derail or switch not properly lined; looking out for broken rail; not exceeding 20 MPH.

block signals, they must restrict their speed, since they need to be able to stop the train within half of the range of sight. In bad weather, this tends to slow train speeds substantially, making it inconvenient for shippers as well as for motorists caught at railroad crossings. The ICC "jury" is still out on this issue. Yet logic suggests that even if the quaint semaphore system survives this round, its days are probably numbered.

Of greater concern is the possibility that a significant portion of the Siskiyou Line may fall to abandonment. The 32.4-mile stretch of track between Glendale (MP 507.9) and Cornutt (MP 540.3) has long been rumored to be in jeopardy. This is owing to two factors. First, serious washouts have occurred along this segment in the past because the tracks parallel Cow Creek through especially difficult terrain. There is reason to believe that if there is any further severe damage, SP may simply close the segment. The other consideration, reasonably enough, is that there are no shippers along this mileage. Already, all the sidings, as well as the signals, have been removed between Cornutt and Glendale, which is not a good sign for the future.

A decision to eliminate the Cow Creek trackage would effectively mark the end of the Siskiyou Line, leaving two dead-end spurs—one from Black Butte to Glendale, and another from Springfield Junction to Cornutt. On the optimistic side, however, SP could retain the Siskiyou Line as a valuable alternative route in the event of a catastrophe on the Cascade Line. A particularly bad derailment or other damage to the primary north-south trunk would be much less troublesome with a substitute route ready to serve.

Interestingly, over the entire 300-plus miles of the Siskiyou Line, there is only one SP branchline—the 5.8-mile White City Branch at Tolo, about nine miles north of Medford. Customers on the branch include Boise Cascade and Down River Forest

A Southern Pacific train at Cow Creek on the Siskiyou Line, January 30, 1986.
Photo: Ed Austin, Collection of Tom Dill.

Products, and, as is so often the case in western Oregon, shipments of lumber are the only thing keeping the rails shiny. Maximum speed on the line is 20 mph, and the route is in relatively good shape, with 112-lb. rail and solid roadbed. The White City Branch is one of only three SP branches in Oregon considered "Secure" in its entirety by the Oregon Public Utility Commission. (The Newberg Branch and the Toledo Branch are the other two.) Every other SP branch in the state has at least a portion of its mileage in a lesser category.

The isolated feeder line provides a link to the WCTU Railway in White City, one of three short-line railroads connecting with the Siskiyou Line. The WCTU is a terminal switching road that handles a variety of shippers in the Medford Industrial Park in White City, and is currently owned by Marmon Industrial Corporation, based in Chicago. WCTU is responsible for moving all freight into and out of the industrial complex, one of Oregon's largest. Steady customers include Husky Charcoal, Boise Cascade, and the 3M Company. In addition, WCTU has a contract to switch several customers along SP track

White City Branch (SP)
Stations

Tolo	MP 450.5
White City	MP 455.9
End of branch	MP 456.3

WCTU Railway
Locomotive Roster

WCTU #5117, GE 70T Switcher (ex-SP, built 1951)
WCTU #5119, GE 70T Switcher (ex-SP, built 1955)

in White City. Besides all of this business, the WCTU also has a fleet of 2,700 boxcars, many of which are leased out to shippers nationwide to provide a bit of extra revenue. These are "railroad brown" cars with WCTR reporting marks; they're usually common sights in the consists of Oregon freights.

The WCTU started business in 1950 as the White City Terminal & Utility Railroad, and owns 12.2 miles of primarily 75-lb. industrial track. Later, the

Union Tank Car Company purchased WCTU, and brought in two GE diesel 70T switchers to better serve its shippers. Previously, the carrier operated with two gasoline-powered Plymouth engines.

Far to the north, another Siskiyou Branch short-line is the 16.4-mile Oregon, Pacific & Eastern, based at Cottage Grove, about 20 miles south of Eugene. At its height, this 1904-vintage line extended 20 miles, from Cottage Grove to Disston. The OP&E is now entirely owned by Bohemia, Inc., the big lumber company that operated two mills at end-of-track in Culp Creek. Bohemia bought out Kyle Railroad's 51 percent share of ownership in 1987.

Oddly, Bohemia undercut its own railroad. Much lumber traffic was trucked from the Culp Creek mill to a reload center on the Burlington Northern in Eugene. It's hard to fault them for this, considering that the reload rate on the BN was about $400 per car less than shipping directly by rail from Culp Creek. The number of carloads held fairly steady in recent years, and, in fact, increased slightly from 1,248 in 1986 to 1,435 in 1988. But on May 15, 1990, Bohemia closed its lumber-planing mill in Culp Creek, idling 29 employees. An adjacent sawmill briefly continued in operation until September 1990 when it too closed, leaving most of the line devoid of customers. Because of the mill closures, tonnage on the line dropped sharply. In 1990, OP&E moved a

total of only 244 freight cars. In 1992, the figure fell to a paltry 66. The OP&E now is controlled by a business called the Row River Investment Company.

Due to these developments, the Oregon, Pacific & Eastern may soon follow the fate of the Boise Cascade-owned Valley & Siletz Railroad. For the immediate future, the OP&E has decided to keep the route to Culp Creek intact and use it to store freight cars, but only one on-line customer remains—Starfire Lumber Company in Cottage Grove—and only about two miles of OP&E's track remains in steady operation. The OP&E plans to continue operations at its freight-car repair facility in Cottage Grove, directly alongside the Siskiyou Line. Cars coming off the OP&E are handled by SP's Yoncalla Local out of Eugene. Before the closure of the Bohemia mills, the level of freight service on the old line was thrice-weekly, and trains were powered by either an Alco S2 or an EMD SW8, the two remaining locomotives in the OP&E stable.

The OP&E is perhaps best known for Hollywood films made on its right-of-way. *The General* and *Emperor of the North* were shot around Cottage Grove on OP&E track. For years, too, the shortline operated a slow excursion train to Culp Creek and back, a 34-mile round trip, featuring a diesel locomotive on weekdays and a Baldwin 2-8-2 steamer on weekends. That service ended in 1988 after 16 years in business, and virtually all of the passenger equipment subsequently was sold or scrapped.

The third shortline that joins the Siskiyou Line is the Yreka Western Railroad, headquartered in Yreka, California, in the inspiring presence of snow-covered 14,162-foot Mount Shasta. One of Willis Kyle's roads, this tiny carrier owns about nine miles of 75-lb. track extending east from Yreka. It joins with the SP at Montague, California—54 railroad miles south of Ashland. Fitting the Siskiyou Line profile, the Yreka Western hauls lumber and woodchips almost exclusively. The line was built in 1889, and currently has two EMD SW8 switch engines for freight movements.

The Yreka Western hosts the "Blue Goose" excursion trains from Yreka's depot to Montague, a "historic railroad and cattle town," according to the carrier's promotional brochures. A steam-powered excursion train runs on weekends, using the same

This early photo shows WCTU #5117 switching in White City. The locomotive is ex-SP #5117, a GE 70-tonner.
Photo: Jack Holst, Collection of PNWC—NRHS.

Oregon, Pacific & Eastern Railway
Locomotive Roster

OPE #21, Alco S2 (built 1941)
OPE #602, EMD SW8 (built 1952)

Yreka Western Railroad
Locomotive Roster

YW #18, Baldwin 2-8-2 (built 1914; out of service)
YW #19, Baldwin 2-8-2 (built 1915)
YW #20, EMD SW8 (built 1953)
YW #21, EMD SW8 (built 1953)

1915 Baldwin Mikado (2-8-2) locomotive (YW #19) that previously handled OP&E excursions out of Cottage Grove. One of the switching diesels works weekday runs.

Rich in lore, and featuring wonderfully named Western towns such as Wolf Creek and Weed along its path, the century-old Siskiyou Subdivision faces a questionable future. Will the 1990s see the abandonment of segments of this once-famous line? Will the line be sold or leased to a new operator? Will the semaphore signals be removed? Will changes in the forest products industry lead to the closure of a number of lumber mills on the line?

All that is certain is that—for now—Southern Pacific's evolving Siskiyou Line offers a magnificent and multifaceted slice of Western railroading.

Above—Oregon, Pacific & Eastern #602 at Cottage Grove, July 27, 1993.

Below—Yreka Western Alco switcher #603 at Yreka, California, August 1969.
Photo: Jack Holst, Collection of PNWC—NRHS.

CHAPTER 9

NO SOOT, NO CINDERS

*Burlington Northern's Oregon Electric Branch
and Astoria Branch*

Like SP's Siskiyou Line, the Oregon Electric Railway was first envisioned as a heavy-duty mainline linking Oregon and California. Although the Siskiyou trackage enjoyed temporary glory as a primary main, the Oregon Electric never made it to California. In fact, stymied by its rival, the Harriman system, it never even extended south of Eugene.

Early in the 20th century, both the Union Pacific and Southern Pacific were owned and controlled by Edward Henry Harriman, and he did not care for competition. At the time when the Oregon Electric started developing its "Willamette Route," Harriman held a virtual monopoly on the movement of goods and passengers through the Willamette Valley corridor. However, the Oregon Electric soon laid rail south from Portland, reaching Salem in 1908 and Eugene in 1912. To Harriman, the encroachment to this point was bad enough, and by no means did he intend to stand by and watch the OE extend all the way to California. Shrewdly, Harriman and the Southern Pacific bought up prime real estate south of Eugene in order to prevent Oregon Electric's southward expansion.

On the other side of this confrontation stood James J. Hill, the famed "Empire Builder" who controlled an equally impressive railroad system, including the Great Northern, the Northern Pacific, the Chicago, Burlington & Quincy, and the Spokane, Portland & Seattle, as well as the fledgling Oregon

Electric. When it became apparent that access out of Eugene to the south was being effectively blocked by Harriman, Hill looked further east for a right-of-way to California.

(Consequently, the Hill forces built the Oregon Trunk Railway, which opened a 151.5-mile line from Wishram, Washington, to Bend, Oregon, in 1911. Two decades later, the Great Northern successfully consummated its incursion into California with the laying of a 234-mile segment between Bend and Bieber, California (via Klamath Falls, Oregon), in 1931. This trackage is now known as BN's Bieber Line, or "Inside Gateway." At Bieber, the line connects with Union Pacific's ex-Western Pacific mainline. Taken as a whole, the Wishram-Bieber through-route stretches 385 miles, and includes 75.4 miles of trackage rights over SP's Cascade Line between Chemult and Bieber Line Junction (Klamath Falls). Along the way, a Burlington Northern branch extends 34 miles west from Lookout (12.7 miles north of Bieber) to Hambone, California, where it connects with shortline McCloud River Railroad.)

Meanwhile, long before Great Northern gained entry into California, the Oregon Electric Railway— acquired as a subsidiary by the SP&S in 1910—had completed its destined southward extension in western Oregon and arrived in Eugene on October 15, 1912. Local excitement was infectious.

"The greatest day in the history of Eugene," boldly proclaimed one newspaper. A specially built, fancily painted welcoming arch (over Willamette Street at Sixth Avenue) greeted the train. The arch was adorned with promotional slogans such as "One more spoke in Albany's hub," and "More prosperity for Portland."

Burlington Northern SW1000 #378 works the industrial district at the southern end of the Oregon Electric Branch in Eugene as storm clouds rise in the distance, July 20, 1990. The stop sign just in front of the surprisingly clean switcher protects SP's Coos Bay Branch.

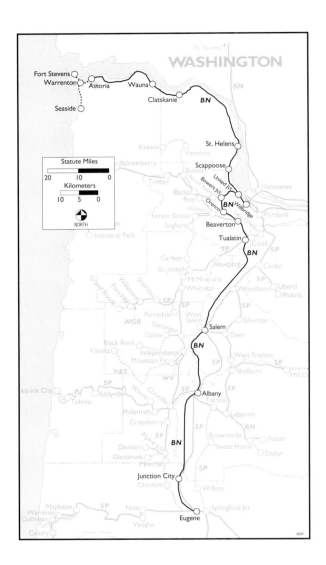

*Burlington Northern's Oregon Electric Branch
and Astoria Branch*

Early in the 1900s, there was tremendous interest in the development of electric trains, which were powered by overhead electric trolley wire instead of coal- or wood-fired engines. This was the innovative "clean energy" of the day, and passengers proved enthusiastic about OE's use of electrics. Before the introduction of electric trains, smoke, soot, and cinders blowing back from locomotives sometimes left travelers gritty and their clothes blackened. Thus, the coming of the electric train was greeted with delight, for it truly did represent an upgrade in service.

Partly in response to Oregon Electric's success with its interurban trains, SP initiated its own "Red Electric" passenger service. These were electrified cars that, logically enough, were painted an elegant red. The Red Electrics began service in 1914, reaching throughout the Willamette Valley. (By the end of the 1930s, however, most of Oregon's electric interurban passenger service would be gone. A remnant from earlier times—the former Oregon Electric depot in Eugene—has now been turned into the fine Oregon Electric Station restaurant and is listed on Oregon's register of historic places.)

At its peak, five Oregon Electric passenger trains

Above—A Southern Pacific "Red Electric" train near Bertha, September 30, 1928.

Photo: Del Burckhardt, Collection of Oregon Historical Society, #DB 303.

Left—BN SW1000 #388 in Eugene, at the end of the Oregon Electric Branch. The switcher is crossing SP's Coos Bay Branch, May 20, 1988.

a day were scheduled between Eugene and Portland, making the run in three and a half hours. On SP's parallel line, travel time between the same cities was four hours. By way of contrast, service on Amtrak in the 1990s between Eugene and Portland—now reduced to one train per day in each direction—takes 2 hours and 59 minutes northbound, and 2 hours and 36 minutes southbound, according to the Amtrak timetable effective through October 24, 1992.

Passengers on the Oregon Electric could also travel directly to Corvallis on a five-mile branchline extending due west from Gray to an OE station at East Corvallis, on the east bank of the Willamette River. Gray was situated on the OE main about halfway between Fayetteville and Albany. This line was abandoned in the early 1930s.

In the 1990s, the 132.3-mile Oregon Electric Branch—United Junction to Eugene—is Burlington Northern's access to western Oregon's population and industrial centers. The Oregon Electric line is formally regarded as BN's 8th Subdivision of the Portland Division.

Despite its role as a major trunk line from which other BN branches radiate (the Santiam Branch, Vernonia Branch, and Astoria Branch all directly connect), the Oregon Electric is comparatively lightly built. From Salem to Eugene (73 miles), the line is comprised of mostly 75-lb. jointed rail, with some 90-lb. Ballasting is crushed rock, but many ties are aging and splitting apart. Between Salem and United Junction, the roadbed is somewhat better, with 112-lb. jointed rail in place over most of this 59-mile section. In addition, a tie replacement program was undertaken in 1989 and 1990 on much of the route.

Notwithstanding the Oregon Electric's light track, trains are allowed to speed along, relatively speaking. The Federal Railroad Administration rates the line as Class 2 and Class 3, permitting freight train speeds of 25 mph to 40 mph, respectively. BN's own directives specify that trains may travel at 35 mph between United Junction and Albany, and 25 mph between Albany and Eugene.

An interesting aspect of the OE's construction was that the company insisted upon laying track in a virtual straight line up the valley wherever possible. There are relatively few curves, and some that do exist today are there only because political jurisdictions pressured the railroad to relocate tracks to benefit developers. In the 1980s, for example, the city of Salem wanted to repair and widen streets through its turf, and so the BN tracks were curved this way and that to accommodate the city's designs—for better or worse. Now, absurdly, the city wants the railroad out *in toto* so it can "develop" the Willamette River waterfront.

Albany Yard on Burlington Northern's Oregon Electric Branch, June 1991.

Traffic levels are consistently high on the Oregon Electric Branch. Trains haul a healthy mix of commodities, although roughly 68 percent of shipments are wood and paper products according to Oregon Department of Transportation figures. There are a large number of forest products firms along the north-south route, plus a General Motors auto parts facility in Beaverton, a Great Western Chemical plant in Tigard, PayLess Drug Store's distribution center in Wilsonville, and several food processing companies (Truitt Bros., Liquid Sugar, Wilsey Food) and a major lumber reload facility in Salem. There are also a number of agricultural shippers that move grass seed outbound, and feed and fertilizers inbound, especially on the trackage south of Albany.

A typical BN freight train working north or south on the segment between Albany and Eugene is almost invariably headed by one unit—usually a GP38-2, although sometimes a GP9 is used—pulling about 30 cars. Consists comprise gondolas loaded with scrap steel, lumber flatcars and boxcars, wood-chip cars, covered hoppers carrying agricultural goods and cement mix, and tank cars containing liquefied petroleum gas and chlorine. Major customers include Sessler, Inc., (scrap steel) at Eugene; Seneca Sawmill Company, also in Eugene; States Industries (veneer) at Enid, four miles north of Eugene; Trus Joist Corporation (laminated wood products) at Junction City; Hunton's Seed Warehouse, Junction City; Hayworth Seed Warehouse at Harrisburg; Morse Bros., Inc., (pre-stressed concrete) at Harrisburg; and James River Corporation (paper products) at Halsey.

Burlington Northern's operations in western Oregon remain one of the last holdouts of waycars. Almost all trains on the Oregon Electric Branch, both local and through movements, still use them; the only exception is weekday Train 482—the Salem to Beaverton local.

The Oregon Electric branch parallels Southern Pacific's Valley Line for almost its entire length. As a result, there has been discussion now and then that BN will abandon segments of its line in favor of trackage rights over SP's main. Specifically, BN has negotiated to use the SP line to Beaverton (via Cook on SP, where the Tillamook Branch joins with the Newberg Branch) instead of by way of its United Junction/Cornelius Pass track. From Cook, BN

Oregon Electric Branch (BN)
Stations

United Junction	MP 10.0
Tunnel Spur	MP 14.6
Bowers Junction	MP 17.1
Merle	MP 20.8
Beaverton	MP 26.4
St. Marys	MP 26.8
Greton	MP 31.3
Tigard	MP 32.1
Wilsonville	MP 42.8
Curtis	MP 45.6
Bush	MP 68.6
Salem	MP 69.0
Minto	MP 72.6
Sidney	MP 84.6
Albany	MP 96.5
American	MP 117.1
Junction City	MP 128.8
Eugene	MP 141.8

would basically like to have rights over SP all the way to Albany. If BN and SP reach such an agreement, pieces of the OE could be dismantled. However, the latest word is that SP is not eager to provide these rights to BN, and negotiations are on hold.

Prospects for the future of BN's Oregon Electric Branch break down like this:

- Eugene to Albany appears safe for the immediate future; there are no plans to alter operations on this 46-mile section. A meeting on February 23, 1993, between BN and shippers on this part of the line resulted in a promise by BN to take no action, for at least a year, that would lead to reduced service. Rail users in the area were concerned about rumors that BN might be planning to abandon 37 miles of track between Albany and Harrisburg.

- Albany to Salem is considered endangered; if BN can secure operating rights over SP, this line could be pulled up.
- Salem to Beaverton is in question. BN would like to reroute its through trains over SP track, while keeping the Oregon Electric open as a feeder route only for local trains.
- Beaverton to United Junction is likely to be abandoned if BN can get running rights on SP. There are not many shippers left along this section, and the difficult grades (e.g., the tremendously high and long wooden trestle at Bowers Junction, and the 4,111-foot-long Cornelius Pass tunnel) demand that additional motive power be employed to move heavy-tonnage freights.

In light of this, the Oregon Electric's existence as a connected line can, on one hand, be considered as tentative. Yet service has held fairly steady over the past few years, and according to Ron Clott, BN's trainmaster in Albany, no trains are in line for termination.

Local switchers are based in four key stations along the branch: at Eugene, MP 141.8; Albany, MP 96.5; Salem, MP 69.0; and Beaverton, MP 26.4. The busy classification yard in Albany is unquestionably the focus of BN's operations on this line. A switch engine, usually an SW1500 or an SW1000, is on duty at the yard almost constantly, sorting cars for various local and through trains. Albany crews prepare a train that travels from Albany to Eugene and back six days a week, excepting Sunday. This freight, officially Train 488, is known as the "Hauler." Albany is also home base to Train 481, a weekday local working the Santiam Branch between Albany and Foster.

To handle the flow of cars in and out of Albany, a through train (number 663 westbound, 664 eastbound) leaves Pasco, Washington, every day at about 8 a.m. headed for Albany, more than 300 miles to the west. Because Train 663 originates in Pasco, well to the east of the Portland-Albany corridor, trains running south on the Oregon Electric Branch from

United Junction to Albany are considered "west-bounds." These trains, normally powered by three or more road units (frequently GP39-2s), are the longest and heaviest operating on the Oregon Electric. They run west to Albany primarily with empties, and leave the Albany yard around midnight on the return trip, hauling mostly loads that have been gathered by local crews on the OE and the Santiam Branch.

Down the line in Eugene, BN's local switcher—generally an SW1000—is active five days a week handling the many on-line industries in the area as well as assembling cars for the return trip of the Albany-Eugene Hauler. In Salem, sidings and yard tracks are often packed with cars; BN does substantial business here, much of it lumber-related. For example, the Cascade Warehouse reload center, located directly behind the modern BN station, is normally filled with center-beam flatcars. A Salem-based crew employs a GP38-2 to serve area customers, including Boise Cascade's paper mill and a cannery across the Willamette River in West Salem, before setting out with an afternoon turn to Beaverton, five days a week. Cars northbound from Salem are usually left in Bush Yard, north of the BN station, to await pickup by the daily Albany-Pasco manifest freight. South-bound cars are left on the siding at Minto, south of Salem.

BN trains now serve West Salem on a piece of what was formerly SP's Dallas Branch. Previous to 1980, the Dallas Branch began on SP's Valley Line at MP 718.3—almost precisely the current location of the Amtrak station in Salem—and went west from there across the campus of Willamette University to reach the Boise Cascade paper mill. The line crossed the Oregon Electric Branch near the mill and continued west on a bridge across the Willamette River to West Salem, eventually going as far as Dallas (a total of 15.5 miles from Salem). BN took over handling Boise Cascade and West Salem customers when a 1.4-mile section of SP's track between the mill and the Amtrak station in Salem was abandoned in 1978. The route of SP's ex-Dallas Branch has been removed west of West Salem (MP 720.5), with what remains of the Dallas Branch starting up again at Thielsen (MP 728.5).

In Beaverton, meanwhile, every morning begins with a GP38-2 or GP9 switching out cars at the GM

Above—Salem is Oregon's capital and third largest city; also it is the approximate halfway point on BN's 132-mile Oregon Electric Branch, and one of four key switching stations along the route. On August 22, 1990, the weekday Salem to Beaverton turn, headed by GP38-2 #2095, waits to roll north out of Salem.

Left—South of Scappoose, on BN's Astoria Line, the daily St. Helens Turn from Vancouver, Washington, leads southbound after delivering cars to the small yard at St. Helens, August 8, 1990. BN GP38-2 #2103 leads leased GP38-2 #747 and a long train back to Vancouver.

Above—A Burlington Northern freight rolls across the trestle at Bowers Junction in 1973. The mixed power on the point includes BN Alco RS3 #4078, formerly SP&S #98.
Photo: Dave Astle.

Above right—On October 12, 1990, northbound Train 488, the "Hauler," sweeps alongside tall weeds as it pulls out of Halsey after switching the James River Corporation's pulp and paper mill. GP38-2 #2259 shows off a new paint scheme rarely seen on Oregon branchlines.

Below right—An Oregon Electric Branch local is northbound at Junction City sometime in 1974. Alco RS11 #4197 does the pulling.
Photo: Dave Astle.

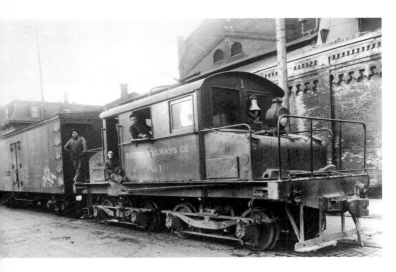

The interurban electric United Railways #1, in the early years of the line's existence.
Collection of Oregon Historical Society, #4.52082.

plant. After this is finished, on Mondays, Wednesdays, and Fridays the local heads over to Forest Grove. On Tuesdays and Thursdays, the same engine and crew serve customers in North Plains and interchanges cars with the Port of Tillamook Bay Railroad.

Sixteen miles north of Beaverton is United Junction, named in recognition of United Railways, one of BN's many predecessors. In 1909, United Railways opened 28 miles of interurban electric passenger line linking Portland to Wilkesboro; this track eventually extended to Keasey, by way of Vernonia, and later became a key part of the Vernonia Branch. United Railways was absorbed by SP&S in 1943.

United Junction, located near Linnton, is also where two important BN lines diverge. The Oregon Electric Branch goes south from there, while the Astoria Branch (7th Subdivision, Portland Division), heads northwest to where the track now ends in Astoria. Service on much of the 95.4-mile Astoria Branch (Willbridge-Astoria) has declined noticeably in recent years. In the 1970s, the yard in Astoria was a much more active place. A switching crew based there worked along the line to Clatskanie and back five days a week, and the solid brick-block depot saw road crews coming and going.

The Astoria Line is former Spokane, Portland & Seattle Railway trackage. As late as the mid-1970s, several years after the Burlington Northern merger, it was not unusual to see daily trains out of Astoria headed by two locomotives often still dressed in

SP&S colors. But Astoria-based service ended in the late 1980s, and now the grand depot is no longer a depot, but a boat repair facility. And the yard sits dormant.

The last lumber mill in Astoria—Astoria Plywood Corporation—closed its doors on February 6, 1991, idling 153 workers, which further threatened the economic viability of the already-fragile western end of the branchline. Astoria Plywood, situated about a half-mile east of the old depot, warranted a train two times a week—on Mondays and Thursdays—and sent out as many as 15 boxcars of lumber weekly. The mill, built in 1951, is being offered for sale, but whether a buyer will materialize is questionable. As of early 1993, it is not being operated. This situation is certain to compound the economic woes of Clatsop County, and is reflected in the unemployment rate in the county, which in June 1992 was 7.6 percent.

For all effective purposes and despite its unlimited potential, the always-promising Port of Astoria is not a user of the rail link to Portland. Proposals over the years to revitalize Astoria's port have included placement of a major grain or coal export terminal there, and more recently an automobile transloading facility. In 1989, there was a great deal of excitement over the latter project, pushed by Consolidated Automotive Resource Service, Inc. (CARS). Plans called for an import/export facility to begin handling up to 200,000 autos yearly, to be moved by rail to the Midwest. But, as of 1993, there are still no automobile shipments coming or going into Astoria, and thus, no trains to move them. Most ocean-going, automobile-carrying vessels continue to call at Portland, Tacoma, and Seattle; yet Astoria remains a viable alternative, in part because it is the closest West Coast port for ships coming from Asia.

In other non-developments, entrepreneur John Gray of San Francisco wanted to buy and operate the Oregon Electric and Astoria branchlines, but lawsuits related to impacts on labor unions put that idea on hold. Gray saw potential for hauling petroleum products, woodchips, garbage, rock, and chlorine by aggressively courting business away from the trucking firms currently handling this traffic.

None of these ideas have taken shape. But perhaps proposals like these are the only thing that has kept the yard in Astoria intact to date. How long it can

Above—BN's Willbridge Yard in northwest Portland is an important base of operations on the Astoria Branch. On July 27, 1990, a mixed freight powered by SD40-2s #7864 and #6359 has just crossed the Columbia River from Vancouver, Washington, bringing cars for distribution to points on BN's Oregon Electric, Forest Grove, Vernonia, and Astoria branchlines. The busy, well-maintained yard provides a poignant contrast with the all but deserted yard 95 miles away in Astoria.

Left—Spokane, Portland & Seattle Alco PA #869 leads a freight on the Astoria Branch at Willbridge in August 1969.

Photo: Jack Holst, Collection of PNWC—NRHS.

stay in limbo remains in question. There are two remaining customers for BN in Astoria: Cryo-Shield Enterprises, a firm that installs cooling units in refrigerator cars, and Astoria Warehouse Company, which occasionally ships boxcars of canned goods.

In a positive development, the Pacific Northwest Chapter of the National Railway Historical Society operated a special train in October 1990 over trackage that has rarely seen anything except freight business since about 1955. The round-trip excursion journeyed between Portland and Astoria, carrying passengers to and from the Clatsop County Historical Society's annual Oregon Dixieland Jubilee jazz festival in Astoria. Two BN road units, GP38-2 #2096 and GP38 #2075, did the pulling.

Business prospects along the first 23 miles of the Astoria route, Willbridge to St. Helens, are relatively strong, however. Service is daily, and steady enough to warrant the positioning of a local and a switching crew at St. Helens, a town of 7,500 people. A through train from Vancouver via Willbridge Yard in Portland (Willbridge is near the western end of BN's mainline to Pasco and Spokane, Washington) provides a constant flow of freight cars to trackside customers and the small yard at St. Helens. This assignment, Train 495, makes a round-trip between Vancouver and St. Helens six days a week. It is usually pulled by two GP38-2s (often leased units), the apparent "power of choice" for BN in Oregon. St. Helens itself boasts some important customers, including Boise Cascade and Friesen Lumber. Eight miles east of St. Helens, in Scappoose, shippers include Steinfeld's Products Company, a bottler of pickles. Four miles west of St. Helens is a large chemical facility owned by Reichhold Chemical Company. Also, James River Corporation brings in cars of woodchips to its plant at Wauna, about 26 miles from Astoria.

Operations on the western part of the line involves local Train 898, called for 9:30 a.m. It works northwest from St. Helens to Clatskanie five days per week, and, until the closure of Astoria Plywood, went on from there all the way into Astoria on Mondays and Thursdays. Now, service to Astoria is handled on an "as-needed" basis.

As with SP's Coos Bay Branch, trains out of St. Helens bound for Astoria have to cross several swing-

spans en route. One is over the Clatskanie River at MP 62.7; another is located at Blind Slough, MP 84.8; and still another crosses over the John Day River at MP 94.8.

Drawbridges are always potential trouble spots. On July 24, 1989, a train consisting of eight boxcars and a caboose pulled by BN GP9 #1944 failed to halt at the John Day River's open drawbridge, which was protected only by a stop sign. The locomotive dropped head-first into the water. Two crew members in the cab had to swim to shore, lucky to survive unhurt. A bridgetender was on his way to line the bridge for the train at the time of the incident.

Beyond Astoria, the tracks once extended westward to Warrenton on a long wooden trestle over Youngs Bay. This trackage was embargoed in September 1982, and service was never restored, primarily due to the dangerous and deteriorating condition of the 8,184-ft.-long trestle. Estimates to repair the trestle ranged from a minimum of $800,000 to as much as $13 million. Given the fact that there were only two active shippers remaining beyond Astoria, it shouldn't surprise anyone that the railroad was not interested in picking up the tab.

One line out of Warrenton went about 10 miles farther northwest to Fort Stevens, while another branch extended south to Seaside, about 18 miles away. These lines were finally abandoned in November 1985, and subsequently removed.

The Astoria Line's physical plant is FRA Class 2 and 3, with 90-lb. and 112-lb. jointed rail between St. Helens and Willbridge; and 85-lb. to 90-lb. rail from St. Helens to Astoria. The line is ballasted with crushed rock and/or pit run materials, and appears to be well-maintained. The entire branchline has a 30 mph speed limit for all trains.

In the 1890s, the early years of the development of what is now known as the Astoria Line, the Astoria & Columbia River Railroad built from Portland to Seaside with plans to extend south along the entire Oregon coast to California, via Tillamook. But, once again, as had been the case with the Oregon Electric's California dreams, Mr. Harriman stepped in to thwart Mr. Hill. Harriman, whose Southern Pacific Railroad seemingly had designs on everything in sight, financed the Pacific Railway & Navigation Company line between Hillsboro and

Tillamook. With this leverage, Harriman saw to it that the right-of-way was constructed in such a manner that it would be difficult for the Astoria & Columbia River Railroad to build down the coast. Partly as a result of Harriman's tactical moves, the A&CR's proposed line to California was never constructed. The PR&N was swallowed up by SP in 1915, thereby creating SP's Tillamook Line.

The first through trains from Portland came to Seaside in 1898. Even then, tourism was a big drawing card, and the Astoria & Columbia River's boastful advertising played up that theme dramatically, as the text of a display placard reveals:

> The best of all, Clatsop Beach, is reached and skirted for miles by the Astoria & Columbia River Railroad, with parlor car trains from Portland along the Columbia River and through Astoria—that city in the romantic history of which the flags of Spain, France, Russia, Britain and America mingle, over which Astor's men and Hudson's Bay men wrangled, and which was objective to Lewis and Clark.

Another promotional poster framed the attractions of the Astoria Line this way:

> The Scenic Sea Coast Route. Safe, swift and sure. Two trains daily, all rail from Union Depot in Portland to the sea. No delays, no transfers!

The line no longer carries tourists to the ocean, yet freight still moves on a daily basis over much of the old "Scenic Sea Coast Route," and could increase. A determined initiative by the Port of Astoria could revitalize the entire line. Conversely, the closing of the Astoria Plywood mill might doom the western end of the route.

Much of the Oregon Electric Branch, meanwhile, also could succumb if BN and SP reach a new trackage rights agreement that allows BN to use SP's Valley Line. Traffic is steady on the OE overall, but there are new complications with civic development groups that want to eliminate the right-of-way within city boundaries.

As seems to be the story of most branchlines throughout Oregon, the future of Burlington Northern's Oregon Electric Branch, along with the Astoria Branch, is difficult to predict. 🔧—

Photo taken from the cab of SP&S locomotive #800 as it crossed the Youngs Bay drawbridge on the way to Seaside in September 1951. The train is SP&S passenger train #21.
Photo: Carl E. Vermilya, Collection of Oregon Historical Society, #4.80382.

Astoria Branch (BN)
Stations

Willbridge	MP 4.3
Linnton	MP 7.3
Harbor Siding	MP 8.9
United Junction	MP 10.0
Holbrook	MP 12.8
Scappoose	MP 19.9
St. Helens	MP 27.6
Reichhold	MP 31.3
Goble	MP 39.5
Avon	MP 46.8
Mayger	MP 56.1
Clatskanie	MP 62.2
Westport	MP 71.1
Wauna	MP 73.5
Clifton	MP 78.7
Knappa	MP 86.7
Astoria	MP 99.7

EPILOGUE

UPDATES, SUMMER 1993

*Southern Pacific and the Willamette & Pacific Railroad, Molalla Western Railway,
Willamette Valley Railroad, and Willamina & Grand Ronde Railway;
BN's Oregon Electric; Port of Tillamook Bay Railroad; SP's Coos Bay Branch;
and the "Pacific Northwest High Speed Rail Corridor"*

The majority of the research, writing, and photography in *Backwoods Railroads* was finalized in early 1993. The rate at which Oregon's economy and the railroad industry are evolving is amazing. A number of changes in the operations of Oregon's branchline network occurred while *Backwoods Railroads* was being prepared for publication. Outlined here are most of these developments and their impact on lines described in this book.

The most significant event is the entry of the Willamette & Pacific Railroad into Oregon on February 22, 1993. Signing a lease agreement with the Southern Pacific, the Willamette & Pacific began handling operations on several SP branchlines, including all of the West Side Branch, the Bailey Branch, the Toledo Branch, the Dallas Branch, the Willamina Branch, and a 10-mile segment of the Newberg Branch (between Newberg, MP 748.5, and St. Joseph, MP 738.0). The W&P also has trackage rights on the Valley Line between Albany, MP 690.9, and Eugene Yard, MP 649.7, and into SP's Brooklyn Yard in Portland via portions of the Newberg Branch (Newberg-Cook), the Tillamook Branch (Cook-Willsburg Junction), and the Valley Line (Willsburg Junction-Brooklyn). Albany Yard serves as the W&P's base of operations.

Southern Pacific cited high labor costs and inflexible working regulations as reasons why its branchlines in Oregon could not be operated profitably. However, in regard to future cooperation with the W&P, SP stated its goal was to keep these branchlines operational for at least 20 years, feeding carloads onto the SP's main routes. SP will pay a fee to the W&P for every freight car delivered to its mainline.

The Willamette & Pacific is controlled by the Genesee & Wyoming Railroad, a New York-based shortline. Altogether, the W&P has taken over 184 miles of the SP's more than 700 miles of branchline track in western Oregon, and payrolls about 70 workers, nearly 50 of whom are ex-SP employees. With the new arrangement, the West Side Branch between Amity and Derry has been completely cleared of stored boxcars and reopened, and already is seeing limited service.

Bob Melbo, former superintendent of SP's Oregon Division, is general manager of the W&P. According to Melbo, the railroad plans to invest $11 million on capital improvements, including rehabilitation of the track between Amity and Derry. Through service between Albany and McMinnville—via Corvallis—is on the agenda, but trackwork is necessary before the route again will be ready for heavy use. Shippers in isolated rural communities such as McCoy, where the rails had been out of service for several years, are once again moving goods—mostly agricultural products—by train.

W&P uses its trackage rights on SP's mainline between Albany and Eugene to run a daily Eugene Turn, which leaves Albany in the morning, picks up in Eugene, and returns to Albany with cars that later are built into outbound trains. Consequently, the Toledo Hauler now originates in Albany instead of Eugene. In addition, the W&P has based local switchers at five stations—in Albany, McMinnville, Corvallis, Toledo, and Dallas.

Willamette & Pacific Railroad's McMinnville Hauler is Portland-bound, moving eastward between Cook and Lake Oswego on March 13, 1994. GP39-2 #2305 (ex-Santa Fe) is in the lead.

Willamette & Pacific #2314 "McMinnville," in McMinnville, July 1993.

Initially using leased SP SD9s, the W&P has since purchased 17 ex-Santa Fe GP39-2s. The current motive fleet also includes an ex-SP GP9, three leased SP SD9s, and two GP9s from the Louisiana & Delta Railroad. (The Louisiana & Delta is one of Genesee & Wyoming's six-member "family" of railroads, which in addition to the W&P, L&D, and parent G&W, includes the Buffalo & Pittsburgh, the Dansville & Mount Morris, and the Rochester & Southern.) The Willamette & Pacific also currently owns four cabooses of mixed Southern Pacific and Missouri Pacific heritage.

W&P operations are non-union; consequently, labor unions challenged the W&P/SP lease arrangements. In August 1993, however, a federal arbitrator ruled that SP did not violate labor contracts. Many SP employees have taken jobs with the W&P, although at several dollars less an hour than they were making before. The result of the arbitrator's ruling means it is likely that SP will soon seek to lease the Siskiyou Branch and Coos Bay Branch, as well as what is left of the Tillamook Branch, to one or more shortline carriers. Possibly, more of SP's branchline network will wind up with the W&P, and W&P

managers admit negotiations for additional SP property are continuing.

While all this was happening, SP sold its 10.4-mile Molalla Branch (Canby-Molalla) to another new carrier—the Molalla Western Railway—likewise on February 22, 1993. The line was purchased by Dick Samuels, who also owns the 4.3-mile East Portland Traction Company operating between Milwaukie and Portland. (The East Portland Traction line is the remnant of what was once the Portland Traction Company's 22-mile route to Boring.) Samuels' combined shortlines employ six people.

Trains work between Canby and Liberal two or three times a week as needed. Samuels, however, has indicated he may opt to close the southern three miles of the line into Molalla (MP 757.8), and halt operations beyond Liberal (MP 754.6)—where the carrier's two main shippers are located—if business at the end of the line does not increase.

"The amount of business so far doesn't justify keeping it in place," Samuels explains. The Molalla Western needs to move about 55 freight cars a year on that portion of the line for it to remain viable, but between February and August of 1993 it hauled only six. The Molalla Western's sole locomotive is an ex-Burlington Northern switcher built in 1951. Samuels plans to purchase a second switcher, also of BN heritage, to use on the line soon.

A bit further south, SP has leased out several branchlines radiating east from the Valley Line— these include the Mill City Branch, Geer Branch, and West Stayton Branch. These lines, totaling about 88 miles, were leased (again, on February 22, 1993) by the Root brothers—owners of the Willamette Valley Railroad and the Willamina & Grand Ronde Railway—who had a lot less railroading to do after the Willamette Valley lost its single shipper in Independence. Train activity on these three lines originates in SP classification yards in Salem and Albany. To handle the new business, the Roots have expanded their work force to 18 employees, and they now own a total of five active locomotives, including newly purchased ex-SP SD9 #4433 and ex-SP GP9 #3859.

On Burlington Northern's Oregon Electric Branch, significant operational changes have resulted from an accident occurring on May 14, 1993. A southbound train derailed at a trestle near Keizer, about two miles north of Salem, collapsing the bridge and halting through operations. Fortunately, no injuries occurred, and repair work began immediately. However, this work was quickly suspended. Instead, BN's through trains between Portland and Albany began running on SP's Valley Line, and indications are that this will continue; BN is negotiating with SP for permanent trackage rights. As a result of this accident, there may never again be long-haul trains running through on the Oregon Electric Branch from United Junction to Albany, as had been the procedure for many years. Local operations continue, however, with a crew based in Beaverton now working south as far as Hopmere, 5.9 miles north (east by timetable) of Salem.

On the Port of Tillamook Bay Railroad, a new train began operating in August 1993 to serve the Karban Rock, Inc., gravel quarry near Cochran. The "Rock Train" works five days a week, hauling gravel to Hillsboro for crushing. The crushed rock is used for construction, and some will be utilized as ballast on the POTB. To handle the increase in business, the POTB leased two Burlington Northern SD9s and purchased an ex-SP GP9. The "Rock Train" is designed to operate as a 30-car unit, with gravel being hauled in open-top hopper cars.

In other developments concerning the Port of Tillamook Bay Railroad, the Root brothers and Rail West are no longer involved in managing its operations. After taking over the three SP branchlines, the Roots decided they were spread too thin, and officially stepped away from management of the POTB on July 1, 1993. Consequently, long-range planning for rail service on the POTB route now is in the hands of the five-member Oregon-Tillamook Railroad Authority. Its membership comprises two POTB and three state officials.

On the Coos Bay Branch, SP lost a good customer when the Davidson Industries sawmill in Mapleton permanently closed its facility, laying off 30 millworkers. The reason cited for the closure is one heard frequently in recent years: logs are in short supply. Timber sales in the Siuslaw National Forest declined from 370 million board feet in 1983 to 4 million board feet in 1992. Even the U.S. Forest Service's Mapleton Ranger District office may be transferred

Willamette & Pacific Railroad
Locomotive Roster (August 1993)

WP #1801, GP9 (ex-SP #3855, built 1959)

WP #1802, GP9 (ex-Louisiana & Delta #1751, built 1956)

WP #1803 "Sherwood," GP9 (ex-Louisiana & Delta #1752, built 1957)

WP #2301 "Albany," GP39-2 (ex-ATSF #3600, built 1974)

WP #2302 "Adair Village," GP39-2 (ex-ATSF #3601, built 1974)

WP #2303 "Amity," GP39-2 (ex-ATSF #3602, built 1974)

WP #2304 "Corvallis," GP39-2 (ex-ATSF #3603, built 1974)

WP #2305 "Dallas," GP39-2 (ex-ATSF #3604, built 1974)

WP #2306 "Dundee," GP39-2 (ex-ATSF #3605, built 1974)

WP #2307 "Independence," GP39-2 (ex-ATSF #3606, built 1974)

WP #2308 "Lafayette," GP39-2 (ex-ATSF #3607, built 1974)

WP #2309 "Philomath," GP39-2 (ex-ATSF #3608, built 1974)

WP #2310 "Monroe," GP39-2 (ex-ATSF #3609, built 1974)

WP #2311 "Newberg," GP39-2 (ex-ATSF #3610, built 1974)

WP #2312 "Sheridan," GP39-2 (ex-ATSF #3611, built 1974)

WP #2313 "Toledo," GP39-2 (ex-ATSF #3612, built 1974)

WP #2314 "McMinnville," GP39-2 (ex-ATSF #3613, built 1974)

WP #2315 "Willamina," GP39-2 (ex-ATSF #3614, built 1974)

WP #2316 "Oregon State University," GP39-2 (ex-ATSF #3615, built 1974)

WP #2317 "Bank of Blue Island," GP39-2 (ex-ATSF #3616, built 1974)

Leased Units

SP #4338, SD9

SP #4344, SD9

SP #4389, SD9

Willamette & Pacific Railroad
Caboose Roster (August 1993)

WP #01 (ex-Missouri Pacific #13819, built 1980)

WP #02 (ex-SP #1943, built 1974)

WP #03 (ex-SP #1947, built 1974)

WP #04 (ex-SP #4757, built 1980)

Looking north at Keizer on BN's Oregon Electric Branch. A derailment here in May 1993 cut the line.

out of Mapleton and consolidated with two other district offices in nearby Florence.

In Toledo, the Wheeler Manufacturing, Inc., sawmill closed in February 1993, but the property apparently will be quickly resurrected. It was purchased—for $1.75 million—by the Siletz Tribal Economic Development Commission in July 1993. The Siletz tribe plans to produce lumber from logs harvested on its private timberlands, and presumably will be shipping finished goods by rail.

A positive political note deserves mentioning. Congressman Al Swift (D-Washington) has taken over as chairman of the House Energy and Commerce Subcommittee of Transportation and Hazardous Materials. Swift, as head of this important committee, will help direct a more favorable governmental policy regarding the railroad industry's handling of passengers and freight. In particular, he has stated that he would like to see the restoration of Amtrak service between Seattle, Washington, and Vancouver, British Columbia. Plans call for this route to be reopened sometime in 1994, in part due to Swift's efforts. Swift's leadership should, indirectly at least, prove beneficial to Oregon's railroads and to the shippers that depend on a healthy transportation network. The same can be said about the 1992 election of Bill Clinton to the presidency. One of his economic objectives calls for rebuilding the nation's physical infrastructure—including the railroads.

A visit to Portland by Amtrak's flashy X2000 demonstration train helped showcase the need for refurbishing the nation's transportation network. The X2000 rolled into Union Station in July 1993, on tour to stir up enthusiasm for a proposed new generation of fast and comfortable trains. Sponsors hope the innovative passenger train will revolutionize rail service in the Northwest, by connecting key cities along a 464-mile route between Vancouver, British Columbia, and Eugene, Oregon—officially known as the "Pacific Northwest High Speed Rail Corridor"—with fast and frequent trains. The route runs through the heart of a region with nearly 8 million people—a population which continues to expand.

"The potential here is tremendous, for a number of reasons," explains Joseph Silien, director of business development for ABB Traction, Inc. (Headquartered in Elmira, New York, ABB designed and built

Molalla Western #801 (ex-BN #99) at Canby, July 30, 1993.

Port of Tillamook Bay Railroad
Locomotive Roster (late 1993)

POTB #101, GP9 (ex-Western Rail Corp.)
POTB #3771, GP9 (ex-SP)
POTB #4368, SD9 (ex-SP)
POTB #4381, SD9 (ex-SP)
POTB #4405, SD9 (ex-SP)
POTB #4406, SD9 (ex-SP)
POTB #4414, SD9 (ex-SP)
POTB #4432, SD9 (ex-SP)

the X2000 for Swedish State Railways, which put a fleet of the high-speed trains into service in 1990.)

"The [Pacific Northwest High Speed Rail Corridor] is full of curves, and the more curves, the better this train performs. Also, the spacing of the population centers and the way people do business along this linear strip makes it a natural for this kind of service," says Silien.

Self-steering axles are one "secret" to this train's capabilities. The axles flex on curves, allowing it to achieve speeds up to 40 percent faster than conventional trains. At the same time, a computerized hydraulic system tilts the cars in the curves. In short, the X2000 incorporates 1990s technology, whereas most of Amtrak's contemporary passenger car fleet is 1970s equipment. Since the new train is designed to operate on existing railroad lines, the project would require much less funding than the celebrated "bullet trains" operating in France and Japan.

"Initially we'll catch tourists, but over time, as we add speed and frequency, we can capture a significant portion of the business market," says Gil Mallery, rail branch manager for the Washington Department of Transportation.

"What we're really looking at is buying people off the highway," adds Robert Krebs, intercity programs coordinator for the Oregon Department of Transportation. "And 69 percent of Oregon's population lives within 30 miles of this rail route."

On August 5, 1993, the Oregon Legislature approved $5 million of Governor Barbara Roberts' initial request of $10.3 million to gear up for high speed rail. If all the required funding for improvements to track, grade crossings, and signal systems is secured (Oregon's total share is reported to be about $450 million), top speed along the line would be 125 mph. Amtrak's current maximum speed between Seattle and Eugene is 79 mph. Future plans call for eventually extending the passenger train service straight south of Eugene, on a route that regularly scheduled Amtrak trains have never followed.

"Roseburg is near the top of the list in all projections for future expansion," says Ed Immel, rail planner for ODOT. Appropriately, if a southward extension of rail passenger service comes, SP's Siskiyou Line—which led the way in a previous century—will be the fast train's route. 🚂

D. C. Jesse Burkhardt
Portland, Oregon
August 30, 1993

X2000 Demonstration Train at Portland, July 7, 1993.

BIBLIOGRAPHY

Austin, Ed, and Tom Dill. *The Southern Pacific in Oregon*. Edmonds, WA: Pacific Fast Mail, 1987.

Culp, Edwin D. *Early Oregon Days*. Caldwell, ID: Caxton Printers, Ltd., 1987.

_____. *Stations West*. Caldwell, ID: Caxton Printers, Ltd., 1972.

Drury, George H. *Historical Guide to North American Railroads*. Waukesha, WI: Kalmbach Publishing Company, 1985.

Elliott, Roy. *Profiles of Progress*. Eugene, OR: privately published [printed by Koke Printing & Lithography], 1971.

Handy Railroad Atlas of the United States. Chicago, IL: Rand McNally, 1948, 1978, 1985, and 1988.

Lewis, Edward A. *American Shortline Railway Guide*. Waukesha, WI: Kalmbach Publishing Company, 1986.

Lucia, Ellis. *Tillamook Burn Country: A Pictorial History*. Caldwell, ID: Caxton Printers, Ltd., 1983.

McArthur, Lewis L. *Oregon Geographic Names*. Portland, OR: Oregon Historical Society, 1982.

McDonald, Charles W. *Diesel Locomotive Rosters*. Waukesha, WI: Kalmbach Publishing Company, 1986 and 1992.

Mills, Randall V. *Railroads down the Valleys: Some Short Lines of the Oregon Country*. Palo Alto, CA: Pacific Books, 1950.

Official Railway Guide (North American Freight Service Edition). New York, NY: International Thomson Transport Press, July/August 1988.

Oregon Atlas & Gazetteer. Freeport, ME: DeLorme Mapping, 1991.

"Oregon Blue Book." Oregon Secretary of State, 1993-1994.

"Oregon Division Timetable." Southern Pacific Transportation Company, October 26, 1980.

"Oregon Rail Plan." Oregon Department of Transportation, 1978, 1980, and 1986.

"Oregon Railroad Branchline Abandonments." Oregon Department of Transportation, July 1985.

"Oregon Rail System Status Memo." Oregon Public Utility Commissioner, November 2, 1987.

"Report of the Governor's Task Force on Rail Line Abandonment." Oregon Public Utility Commissioner, October 1986.

"Seattle Region Timetable." Burlington Northern Railroad, October 25, 1987.

Webber, Bert and Margie. *Railroading in Southern Oregon and the Founding of Medford*. Fairfield, WA: Ye Galleon Press, 1985.

"Western Region Timetable." Southern Pacific Transportation Company, October 29, 1989.

The Newberg Branch at Sherwood, summer 1992.

Photo: Deborah A. Winter.

ACKNOWLEDGMENTS

The author wishes to thank the following:

Glen Lindeman and Keith Petersen, editors, and David Hoyt, design/cartography (WSU Press)
Ron Clott (Burlington Northern Railroad)
Bob and Vickie Steele (Oregon Coastline Express)
Mike Root, David Root, and George Lavacot (Willamette Valley Railroad)
J. David Ingles and Kevin P. Keefe (*Trains*)
Don Gulbrandsen (*Pacific Rail News*)
Mike Schafer (*Passenger Train Journal*)
Lon Lasher, Don Mason, and Dale Jones (Port of Tillamook Bay Railroad)
Dave Astle (Oregon Public Utility Commission)
Tom Dill (for generously sharing sources and photos)
Scott Pirie (Western Region Timetable and Albany switching)
Dick Kester (for tales of the Albany Roustabout)
Walt Grande (Grande Press and photo help from NRHS)
Dave Duncan (Norwester Tours, help with "Celebrities" details)
Bill Montgomery (Brooklyn Yard, Tillamook Branch updates)
Dick Samuels (Molalla Western Railway)
Mike Healy (SP's Eugene Trainmaster; the Siskiyou latest)
Bob Melbo and Bruce Carswell (Willamette & Pacific Railroad)
Bob Krebs (the Amtrak figures)
Kathy Dimond (editorial Thanksgiving)
Mark Bloom and Jennifer Reavis (Tigard star tour, July 1993; "Crowbar" review)
Scott Sparling (Thursdays at the signal towers, and Jackson roots)
Thomas Lacinski (GB&W west from Kewaunee, Wisconsin, in the moonlight)
Phil Lynott ("Southbound" and "Fight or Fall")
Carlos Castaneda (*The Power of Silence*)
Monte K. ("Life is stranger than any of us expected. Enigma rules.")
Mom and Dad (Albinar 80mm-200mm lens, and for everything)
Ron (Atwater's and the 40th visit)
Chris (the lead to "Long White Cadillac")
Oregon Historical Society
National Railway Historical Society, Pacific Northwest Chapter
Cole's Camera in Corvallis (film and developing)
WR-41 (Southern Pacific Transportation Company)
SP's Dawson Local crew
Branchline and shortline train crews everywhere

Special thanks to Claudia Howells of the Oregon Public Utility Commission and Ed Immel of the Oregon Department of Transportation—for updates and verifications and an unyielding affection for Oregon's branchline railroads.

Also thanks to Deborah A. Winter—for help with organizing the maps, for the "Spirit of Oregon" illustration…and for the view of the stars, through the forest.

INDEX